Photo by Linda Wheele

Leonard Downie, Jr., Day City Editor of the *Washington Post*, won the American Bar Association Gavel Award and the Liberty Bell Award of the Federal Bar Association for a series of articles on the Court of General Sessions in Washington, D.C., published in 1966. The series is credited with having led to significant reforms. In 1967 and again in 1968, Downie, who joined the *Post* after he received his M.A. degree in political science and journalism from Ohio State University in 1965, won first place in the Front Page awards for general news reporting that are given by the Washington-Baltimore Newspaper Guild. He was one of three principal contributors to the book *Ten Blocks from the White House: Anatomy of the Washington Riots of 1968,* by Ben W. Gilbert and the *Post* staff (Praeger, 1968).

JUSTICE DENIED

JUSTICE DENIED

The Case for Reform of the Courts

LEONARD DOWNIE, JR.

Chaos, confusion, compromise, and bureaucratic expediency and inadequacy are the ugly realities behind every "justice myth" on which most Americans have been reared. Speedy trial, for example, does not exist—except in courtrooms where the poor and downtrodden are quickly deprived of their legal rights through pretrial deals ("plea-bargaining") that disregard the client's guilt or innocence and trials that are assembly-line travesties of justice. Court fees for filing suits and appealing adverse rulings shut many poor people out of the courthouse entirely, while involvement in a long case can bankrupt a middle-income person. The law and its interpretation by the courts often give those with economic power special rights not enjoyed by debtors, tenants, or consumers.

"On top of all this, even the *image* of justice in the courts today is tawdry," says the author of this broadly informed, thoroughly documented, angry, and disturbing book. "The local courthouse is a haven for vagrants sleeping in the corridors, incompetent lawyers and bail bondsmen swarming about like vultures, and hack political appointees clothed in the robes of justice destroying lives through prejudice, whim, and limited legal

(continued on back flap)

JUSTICE DENIED

The Case for Reform of the Courts

LEONARD DOWNIE, JR.

PRAEGER PUBLISHERS
New York • Washington • London

PRAEGER PUBLISHERS
111 Fourth Avenue, New York, N.Y. 10003, U.S.A.
5, Cromwell Place, London S.W. 7, England

Published in the United States of America in 1971
by Praeger Publishers, Inc.

© 1971 by Praeger Publishers, Inc.

Library of Congress Catalog Card Number: 70–131942

Printed in the United States of America

Contents

5

ability. Through its halls, drunks, tired prostitutes, and trembling heroin addicts are paraded aimlessly, like stale vaudevillians. Criminal suspects, litigants, witnesses, and jurors must wait out seemingly endless delays before their brief moment in court—and then they are rushed along like animals being prodded to slaughter."

Few writers are better qualified to voice such opinions. As an editor and investigative reporter for the *Washington Post,* Leonard Downie, Jr., has been deeply concerned with the shortcomings of the present-day American court system. In the preparation of this book, he traveled thousands of miles, visited scores of courtrooms, and talked to judges, lawyers, and professors of law in his search for the truth about the failings of the courts and for suggestions for both reforming the nation's legal system and restoring to the political system a healthy belief in the rule of law.

His efforts have produced a work of significance for all officials of the city, state, and federal governments, as well as members of the legal profession. It is also a book for anybody who has ever been called or eligible for jury duty, been a defendant in traffic court, rightly or wrongly been arrested on a criminal charge, been sued or brought suit in a civil case. It is for any citizen who has ever been or ever may be faced with an action involving a contemporary court or who is concerned because his faith in American justice is less than strong.

Preface

Somewhere in the United States, in some small city or rural county seat, there must exist a courthouse where trials are held on time for everybody who wants one, where judges and lawyers perform their tasks ably, and where the public is treated courteously and justly. But, in the cities and suburban clusters where the vast majority of Americans live today, one finds mostly chaos, injustice, and cynical indifference in the local courthouses.

It is time that lawyers and judges recognize this fact. It is also time that the American public be fully informed about how badly the courts work, why they work badly, and what changes have been urged by those few brave lawyers who champion reform.

That is what this book is intended to do. I doubt that it could have been written by a lawyer. As a nonlawyer, I am free of the pressures and narrow traditions of the legal profession. Most lawyers learn well in law school the tenet that the U.S. legal system as it is now constituted is the best of all possible systems and should not be drastically changed. Their fear that some disaster might result from radical alteration of the system prevents them from fully appreciating the seriousness of the crisis that now threatens the courts. The few among them who do see clearly the problems usually become so deeply involved in one part of the system, and what might be done to improve that part, that they can scarcely be expected to attempt an overview.

I will not be surprised if many lawyers do not like what is said in this book, because it contests the assurances they give the rest of the citizenry that the laws and courts still produce justice, no matter how compellingly the evidence might indicate the contrary. This book is aimed at piercing the veil of secrecy lawyers try to keep around their work and the courts, so that the reader can see what really goes on and so that he will, perhaps, be stirred into demanding change. Lawyers generally and naturally do not welcome having the problems of the courts and the sins of their profession brought out into the open. When New York's Mayor John Lindsay partly blamed his city's overloaded and badly run courts for riots and suicides in the municipal jails, where too many men had been crowded together for too long awaiting trials, the judiciary expended more energy in sharply criticizing the mayor for speaking out than it did in addressing itself to changes that might alleviate some of the problems. Several judges warned that the effect of what they considered to be an intemperate outburst by the mayor might be a great loss in public respect for the law. What the judges apparently cannot admit is that any citizen who happens into any branch of the criminal court of New York is bound to come away drained of almost all respect for the legal process.

My book is not intended to criticize lawyers, judges, and courthouse employees for the sport of it or to hold them alone to blame for the wrongs visited on millions of citizens in one way or another by the judicial system. Rather, it is written to sound a warning—to lawyers and to laymen—that something must be done, before it is too late, to save our courts from collapsing completely. I believe that it is not too alarmist to contend that at stake is the hope of helping to preserve the nation's Rule of Law.

In its preparation, I spent two years observing big-city court operations through eyes trained by my experience as an investigative reporter for the *Washington Post*, including much time spent examining the problems of the Court of General Sessions in Washington, D.C. In the course of my own research, I visited courts in Cleveland, Detroit, Chicago, Los Angeles, and New York City and interviewed many officials. My book also utilizes every scrap of research into court problems by lawyers, scholars, and newsmen that I could find. I believe that my Bibliography is one of the most complete to date on the topic of court reform—most of the works listed were published within the last five years— and hope that it will lead interested readers into seeking out the more specialized books available on the subject. The conclusions I draw and the reforms I suggest are, for the most part, similar to those that have been put forward by the few lawyers who have been pressing for reform. Until now, however, this material has not been collected and presented in one book intended for the general public.

Obviously, I am deeply indebted, for the pioneering work they have done, to those lawyers and others whose names appear in the Bibliography. In addition, I am particularly grateful to Daniel J. Freed of the Yale University Law School, to former U.S. Senator Joseph D. Tydings of Maryland, to Chief Judge Harold H. Greene of Washington's Court of General Sessions, and to Harry I. Subin of the Vera Institute of Justice in New York, for their personal counsel, instruction, and inspiration over a period of many years. I also want to thank Lois Decker O'Neill, Praeger's Washington editor, who first urged me to consider this book and then guided me with much patience and skill through its realization; Gerry Rebach, who greatly improved the manuscript at various stages with her own editing ability; and Karen Nicola and Mary Haislip for the typing of various drafts and revisions.

Washington, D.C.
February, 1971

JUSTICE DENIED

I

A Nation on the Docket

"Why should there not be a patient confidence in the ultimate justice of the people?"

This rhetorical question, chiseled into the dirty gray sandstone of Manhattan's Criminal Court Building, is answered just inside the doors. New York City's Criminal Court, one of the most crowded and chaotic in a nation full of courts too overwhelmed to provide justice, demonstrates all too plainly that the myths under which the legal system operates in the United States have become cruel jokes.

Every American accused of a serious crime is theoretically guaranteed the right to a trial by jury. But only one of every ten suspects convicted of a serious crime today receives a trial. The rest agree to plead guilty, usually after bargaining for what they think is a favorable sentence.

The U.S. Constitution requires that meticulous due process be followed before any citizen can be deprived of liberty or property; protection of this right has been strengthened by decisions of the Supreme Court and other appellate tribunals. But, every few minutes, the criminal and civil trial courts deny citizens these rights in the rush to satisfy bureaucratic aims with savings of time and money—not, however, the citizen's time or money. The guidelines of Supreme

Court decisions are ignored. Compromise and whim decide more cases than due process.

Justice is supposed to be swift; otherwise, according to legal theory, there is no justice at all. But suspects who insist on trial by jury must wait in crowded, filthy jails for as long as a year or more before their cases are called. Persons injured in automobile accidents must wait two to five years for a judge or jury to decide how much they may collect in damages to pay their medical bills.

The opportunity for justice should be *"equal and exact . . . to all men of whatever state or persuasion"* promises another epigraph on the wall of the court building in New York. But only the rich can afford able lawyers and long court delays. Court fees for filing suits and appealing adverse rulings shut many poor people out of the courthouse entirely, and involvement in a long court case can, like an unexpected illness, bankrupt a middle-income person. The law and its interpretation by the courts often give those with economic power and property special rights not enjoyed by debtors, tenants, or consumers.

In theory, the courts operate under an adversary system whereby the opposing sides strenuously present evidence supporting their claims before an impartial judge and jury. But most civil, as well as criminal, cases end, before trial, in compromise agreements. Only the contested cases, a tiny minority, are reviewed by appellate courts or made the subjects of legal study.

"There are widening discrepancies between the formal law in the books and the law in action in the courts," wrote Columbia University law professor Harry W. Jones in his introduction to *The Courts, the Public, and the Population Explosion.** "These are not cracks to be painted over, but faults that imperil the structure of American justice."

---

* See Bibliography for further information on books cited in text.

What worries many thoughtful men who believe the present time to be particularly perilous for the nation is that more and more citizens today are coming to disbelieve the promise of justice and are turning to violent dissent, advocacy of unconstitutional repression, or mindless lawlessness. They no longer believe that the system will eventually work for them. They no longer have faith in the rule of law.

The dismaying, ugly fact is that disbelief in the efficacy of the U.S. legal system is well founded. Every day, the laws, and the trial courts that administer the laws, deny justice more frequently than they produce it. The courts, beset with archaic methods and chronic shortages of judges, other personnel, and money, have been overwhelmed by a tidal wave of cases. An increasing population, a rapidly rising crime rate, the side effects of the age of the automobile, and a new awareness of the legal problems and rights of poor citizens have combined to double, triple, even quadruple annual numbers of cases in cities across the nation. Chaos is the norm. Delays for individual cases run into years, despite tremendous pressures to break down and compromise claims before the time-consuming trials. When a case does reach a judge, he rushes it through as hastily as possible. In addition to these mechanical evils, class discriminations written into the laws and built into court procedures work against all but well-to-do litigants. The resulting wrongs touch more lives and are communicated faster to the rest of the population today than ever before.

People frightened by an increasing incidence of crime discover that accused criminals seldom go to trial and often are let off with mere slaps on the wrist. Outdated laws, bureaucratic slip-ups, and expedient denial of constitutional due process periodically trap innocent men in the criminal courts and, too often, set the guilty free. Hardened criminals return to society little changed and commit new crimes.

The poor, including a large proportion of urban blacks,

find that they are treated as second-class citizens in court. With laws and procedures favoring the rich, the landlord, the creditor, and the predatory merchant, the very poor and the ordinary working man or woman are often denied basic rights, including even the opportunity to confront those who victimize them. Middle-class citizens, too, are denied justice by the long delays and high costs of court processing. They cannot recover adequate damages when injured in accidents or cheated in business. They must pay an exorbitant legal tariff when obtaining a divorce, buying a new home, or settling the estate of a deceased relative.

On top of all this, even the *image* of justice in the courts today is tawdry. The local courthouse is a haven for vagrants sleeping in the corridors, incompetent lawyers and bail bondsmen swarming like vultures, and hack political appointees clothed in the robes of justice destroying lives through prejudice, whim, and limited legal ability. Through its halls, drunks, tired prostitutes, and trembling heroin addicts are paraded aimlessly, like stale vaudevillians. In its anterooms, criminal suspects, litigants, witnesses, and jurors must wait out seemingly endless delays before their brief moment in court—and then they are rushed along like animals being prodded to slaughter. Noted legal scholar Edward L. Barrett, Jr., has found "scant regard for human dignity and the worth of the individual" in the mass processing of cases in the courts.

The American court system today works no better—and undoubtedly discourages many more citizens with its failings—than did its nineteenth-century British ancestor, Chancery Court, which, as Charles Dickens described it in his novel *Bleak House*, had "its decaying houses and its blighted lands in every shire . . . its worn-out lunatic in every madhouse, and its dead in every churchyard."

How can there be patient confidence in ultimate justice? Justice itself is on trial.

Compare the courts in Chicago, Cleveland, Los Angeles, or any other American city in the 1970's with Dickens's description of Chancery Court,

> which so exhausts finances, patience, courage, hope; so overthrows the brain and breaks the heart; that there is not an honourable man among its practitioners who would not give—who does not often give—the warning, "Suffer any wrong that can be done to you, rather than come here!"

Think of those words on entering, for example, Recorders Court in the city of Detroit. . . .

II

Criminal Court or Sausage Factory?

The elderly lawyer pushed through the swinging gate in the dark wood railing that separates court officials from the public and walked up and down past packed rows of spectators. He was dressed for the race track, where he intended to spend the afternoon, in an orange and green sport coat, bright green slacks, and soft white leather shoes, and his clothes were a flash of unexpected color in the drab, stuffy, downtown courtroom.

It was 10 o'clock on an August morning in Recorders Court, which is the criminal court for the city of Detroit. In many ways, the scene could have been any criminal courtroom in the United States.

"Jackson," the lawyer called out. "Sam Jackson."

He was trying to find a client he had seen only once before, months ago, when he had been appointed to defend the man for a $100 fee paid by the state of Michigan. On that first day, he stood briefly beside his client as Jackson was arraigned and a date was set for his trial. Until this morning, when a courtroom clerk handed him a copy of the official court "paper" for the case, the lawyer had done nothing more.

"Jackson," he called again.

A slightly built black man in a polo shirt and work pants

rose hesitantly a few rows back in the audience. Sam Jackson, a sometime laborer and truck driver, had, his record showed, been connected on and off with gambling and dope. He had been arrested nearly a year earlier for possession of a concealed pistol, which was found when a police detective stopped and searched his car, and he had been free on bail since then, waiting for his trial. That day, he was one of many defendants, mostly black, crowded together with relatives and friends in the worn wooden pews of Courtroom 8.

To these benches and to the barred cells hidden behind the courtroom are brought each day scores of men and women charged with such felonies as murder, rape, robbery, burglary, serious assault, the sale or possession of narcotics, or the illegal possession of a weapon. Many, like Jackson, wait a year or longer to be tried. But, for most of them, trial before a judge and jury never comes.

"Jackson?" the lawyer asked, pushing down his glasses to peer at his client. "Okay, okay. Sit back down. I'll be with you in a minute."

Turning, he walked through the gate again toward a cluster of policemen, all in street clothes, standing and gossiping idly near the empty jury box on the left side of the courtroom. In the confusion and cacophony that characterize the criminal-courtroom scene, the policemen, numbering about thirty, were balanced by a swirling, changing mass of as many men opposite them. These are the criminal lawyers, most of whom work in Courtroom 8 every day. Their only clients, whose fees are usually paid by the state, are those assigned to them by the court. Some keep dingy offices in squat, grimy buildings across narrow Clinton Street from the courthouse; others have no offices at all and operate out of the courtroom itself. Known collectively as the "Clinton Street bar," they carry no brief cases and seldom consult lawbooks; their case preparation consists of marking trial dates in dog-eared date books and scanning court papers hurriedly on the day a case comes up. Jackson's lawyer is one of the more flamboyant Clinton Street barristers.

By this time, as the lawyer passed by, the judge was already seated on his perch atop a two-tiered wooden platform, surrounded by clerks, bailiffs, and other functionaries shuffling through and stamping papers just below him. Save for the two or three persons standing immediately before him to conduct business, nobody seemed really aware of the judge's presence. Lawyers, policemen, clerks, and others criss-crossed noisily in front of his bench, streamed back and forth through the swinging gate, and generally kept up an ocean's roar of conversation that crashed around the pronouncements of the judge, occasionally drowning out his words altogether.

"Detective Sanders," Jackson's lawyer loudly addressed a policeman in a gray suit. "You got the Jackson case?" The policeman, recognizing the attorney from past dealings, nodded. "Good," said the lawyer, still several feet away. Then, ignoring the judge nearby, the lawyer shouted the question that, in Recorders Court, takes the place of trials, juries, legal rules, and the rest: "Hey, Sanders, what can you do for me today?"

Coming together in the middle of the courtroom, the lawyer and policeman began to haggle amiably over what reduction the government might make in its charge against Jackson if he agreed to plead guilty rather than go to trial before a jury. If convicted of the felony charge by a jury, Jackson would be given a prison sentence of several years. The law required it. The policeman suggested to the lawyer that the charge could probably be reduced to "failure to present a gun for licensing," a misdemeanor carrying a penalty of only ninety days in jail, *if* Jackson agreed to plead guilty immediately. Together, the lawyer and Detective Sanders then crossed in front of the judge to join a

line of other attorneys and policemen that stretched to a
back room occupied by the prosecutor—an official who is
himself seldom seen in the courtroom.

Case by case, the prosecutor and each lawyer, usually
joined by the policeman involved, hammer out a bargain
for a guilty plea, similar to the one that Jackson's lawyer
was seeking. If the accused agrees to admit guilt rather
than insisting on a trial by jury, the government reduces the
charge against him, often seemingly assuring the defendant
a lighter sentence. Thus, a man charged with armed robbery, which carries a mandatory twenty-year prison sentence, might plead guilty to unarmed robbery or attempted
robbery and receive a sentence of a few months or years in
prison. Another, charged with burglary, might "admit" to
attempting "unlawful entry." The changes are not made
simply to fit the facts of the crimes involved; usually, in fact,
the robber *had* used a gun or the burglar *had* succeeded in
getting inside a house and carrying off an armful of valu-
ables. Instead, the change is made to induce the defendant
to trade the possibility of a long prison term (against the
chance for freedom if acquitted by a jury) for the promise
of a shorter sentence.

In Sam Jackson's case, the prosecutor readily agreed to
the bargain offered by the lawyer and policeman. The
lawyer came out, found Jackson again, and took him into
the bustling hallway outside the courtroom.

"I got you ninety days," he told Jackson enthusiastically.
He did not refer at all to the crime itself or to his client's actual guilt or innocence. "It's a good deal. You have a record.
You go to trial and get convicted on the felony and you're
in trouble."

Jackson nodded in agreement.

"Remember," the lawyer cautioned as the men started
back inside the courtroom, "don't hem and haw in front of
the judge, or he might insist on a trial."

Jackson's turn came quickly. He stood mute, while the judge, a shrunken man in his sixties, sorted through papers on his desk and read out the defendant's name and address and the charge originally placed against him. A court stenographer recorded everything on a stenotype machine.

"The prosecutor has signed a statement that he will accept your plea of guilty to a lesser charge," the judge announced, in words familiar from uncounted other cases. Then, like a clergyman reading a litany, with Jackson responding at appropriate pauses, he intoned, "You are pleading guilty because you are guilty?"

"Yes, sir."

"No one has threatened you or promised you anything?"

"No."

"No one has induced you to plead guilty?"

"No."

"You understand your constitutional right to a trial, and you are freely waiving that right?"

"Yes."

Turning sideways in his overstuffed swivel chair to stare out a soot-clouded window, the judge wearily recited, as he had again and again already that morning, "Let the record show that counsel was present, that the defendant was advised of his rights and that he understood them, and that the defendant waived his right to trial by jury or this court, and that he freely withdrew his plea of not guilty and entered a plea of guilty."

The court stenographer took down every word. The judge swiveled around again and sentenced Jackson to ninety days in jail.

Plea bargaining is what the lawyers call it.

No trial. No jury of peers. No exhaustive search for truth. No exacting legal rules. Only empty, sometimes dishonest words substituted for the reality of due process guaranteed by the Constitution.

A lawyer who knows next to nothing about his client or the facts of the crime with which he is charged barters away a man's right to a trial, and, along with it, the presumption that a defendant is innocent until proved guilty—the presumption on which the American system of criminal justice rests. A prosecutor who knows little more about the case than what a policeman tells him hurriedly trades off one of American society's most important responsibilities—the responsibility for providing a full hearing for those charged with criminal acts and the levying of appropriate sanctions upon those convicted of crimes against that society. The judge, who has abdicated his authority to bartering lawyers, acquiesces to all this and sanctifies it for "the record."

Everyone pays lip service to justice. But everyone's true faith is in expediency.

And why not? An indifferent public has allowed the system to become overwhelmed with work: too many cases for too few judges, too few lawyers, too few clerks. An uncaring legal community has failed to modernize the system to cope with the inundation. How else can the system survive, except by trying to dispose of cases as fast as it can?

Plea bargaining instead of trials is the answer in crowded criminal courts across the nation. In New York, prosecutor and defense attorney haggle over guilty pleas in front of the judge's bench in frenetic whispers between cases. In Chicago and San Francisco, the bargaining is often carried out in polite confidential conferences, sometimes in the judge's chambers, with his participation. In Washington, D.C., brisk and business-like plea bargaining is conducted in small glass-enclosed cubicles in the prosecutor's office before the case goes to a judge. In Dallas, prosecutors bargain directly with incarcerated defendants through jailhouse bars. According to the best estimates, at least 90 per cent of the persons "convicted" in American courts are never proved guilty at all. Instead, they plead guilty without trials.

Everyone in the system, including the judge and the defendant's own lawyer, offers inducement or exerts pressure for a guilty plea, to save the time and trouble of a trial. If the prosecutor is not empowered to reduce the charge, the judge makes it clear that his sentence will be lighter for a guilty plea. Those who insist on a trial, the most basic of constitutional rights, are openly punished by prosecutors and judges with maximum charges and harsh sentences.

Sometimes, the judge takes a leading role in the bargaining process. In one routine case in Chicago's criminal court, selection of a jury began at 10 A.M. for the trial of a young Mexican American charged with selling heroin to an undercover agent. As the tedious process of interviewing jurors dragged on into late morning, the judge suddenly interrupted and asked the opposing lawyers, "Do you want a conference in this case?"

In Chicago, that is the signal to begin bargaining. The prosecutor and lawyer followed the judge out of the courtroom to his chambers, and, once inside, the prosecutor offered to reduce the charge to possession of heroin. The judge, noting that it would be the youth's second conviction for that offense (in Illinois, where most sentences include both a minimum and maximum time, the maximum for a second narcotics conviction can be life imprisonment), said that he would sentence him to a minimum of five and a maximum of ten years in prison if he would plead guilty.

The defense lawyer, a law professor who frequently volunteers to defend indigent suspects free of charge, refused the deal. "Too much time," he said about the proposed sentence.

"Look," the judge warned him, "if that man is convicted by a jury, I'll give him twenty years. You take some of my time; I'll take some of his."

But the lawyer refused to give in. The three returned to the courtroom. Most of another hour went to interviewing jurors, and lunchtime neared. The prosecutor called the lawyer over with him to the judge's bench, saying in an anxious undertone, "Look, I'm busy. I've got another case to be tried this afternoon. How about two to ten years?"

The judge inclined his head in agreement. But the defense lawyer countered with two to five years, because reduction in the maximum end of the sentence can mean earlier parole. The judge thought a moment, grimaced, and gave in. The defendant pleaded guilty.

Most often, a prosecutor starts off the plea-bargaining process by charging defendants in ways designed to produce compromises. In Cleveland, Ohio, and Washington, D.C., for instance, a defendant is regularly charged with a slew of offenses covering a single crime: A bank robber is indicted for armed robbery, theft, one charge of assault with a deadly weapon for every customer and teller he pointed his gun at, possession of an illegal weapon, and so on. In California, under a strange old law, a technical charge of kidnaping is thrown in for good measure if the robber orders victims at gunpoint to move around, lie down, or open a safe. If the defendant in these or similar situations pleads guilty, all the charges but one are dropped. What happens if he chooses not to plead guilty? In Cleveland, if a defendant insists on a trial and is convicted, the judge often metes out for each charge separate sentences that must be served one after the other. Under Ohio's law for minimum-maximum sentences, this practice leads to such absurdities as a sentence of twelve to 240 years in prison (one to twenty years for each of twelve charges) given a woman convicted of embezzling union funds.

In places where the prosecutor habitually levies only one charge for a crime, usually the strongest suitable for the circumstances, prosecutors and defense attorneys—especially public defenders who are also paid by the government and work alongside the prosecutor in court every day—operate on informal understandings that certain charges will always be reduced to certain lesser offenses. In California, for instance, according to a recent study by the University of California Center for Legal Studies, "burglary" is usually reduced to "petty theft," "assault with a deadly weapon" to "assault without a weapon," and "molesting children" to "loitering at a school playground." (In cities like Detroit and Chicago, where a charge of armed robbery frequently becomes one of unarmed robbery if the defendant pleads guilty, the decision to plead is called "swallowing the gun.") In Washington, D.C., the distinction between a plea for felonious assault and one for simple assault, which is a misdemeanor, often is based on the number of stitches required to close the victim's wounds. In New York City, four of every five defendants originally charged with a felony wind up pleading guilty to a misdemeanor.

"We are running a machine," a Los Angeles prosecutor has told one researcher. "We know we have to grind them out fast." A Chicago prosecutor uses the same words, vowing, "I'll do anything I can to grind them out fast." So, frequently, will the defendant's own lawyer, whether he is a public defender or is privately retained, with the result that, on almost any day in a big city's criminal court, a defendant can be seen disavowing before a judge a guilty plea arranged by his lawyer.

In such a typical case on a typical day in San Francisco's Superior Court, three defendants in a burglary case were supposed to plead guilty in exchange for being placed on probation. Their lawyers had made the arrangements with the judge in his chambers. But, when the defendants themselves came before the judge from the lockup, one insisted that he was not guilty. "This is not what I expected," his lawyer, a public defender, said sheepishly, as the judge ordered a date set for a trial. On the way out of the courtroom, the public defender apologized to the lawyers for the other two defendants that their scheme had gone awry.

"The best-laid plans of mice and men," he muttered. "That guy doesn't know what's good for him."

In Detroit's Recorders Court, where only three of every hundred criminal defendants is ever tried by a judge or jury, the plea-bargaining system is merely a little more overt than it is elsewhere. Once a deal is made, every formal rule and safeguard is blatantly twisted to accommodate it. Thus, on the same morning that Sam Jackson made his guilty plea for failure to present a gun for licensing, a man charged with burglary decided to plead guilty to attempted unlawful entry. He was questioned by the judge about when and where the crime took place, as Michigan law requires if there is any doubt about accepting the plea in lieu of trial.

"Where did the offense occur?" the judge asked.

The defendant was silent. Clearly, he did not know or could not remember. The judge picked up a police report and read off an address. "Is that the one?" he asked.

"Yeah, that sounds like it," the man answered.

The judge then read off a time, a date, and a list of items stolen from the house identified. The defendant said it all seemed to sound right. The judge accepted his plea.

On another day, another judge, G. W. Crockett, asked a twenty-year-old with a bushy Afro hair style why he was pleading guilty.

"To get off," the youth answered matter of factly.

"What?" demanded Crockett, a black man who has been something of a dissenter and unsuccessful reformer in Detroit's Recorders Court.

"I want to get probation," the young man said. "I want to get out of jail." He had been imprisoned 150 days awaiting trial. "They said I could get out this way, that you'd give me probation. Besides, I didn't really rob anybody. I just took some reefers off that woman's bed. I was visiting there. We were friends. I just slipped them out. I didn't pull any knife like they said."

Crockett, an ebony-skinned man with graying hair, shook his head. The youth had been charged with armed robbery. The prosecutor decided to allow him to plead guilty to larceny, a misdemeanor, so that he would be eligible for probation or a sentence of only a few months in jail, instead of twenty years in prison.

"I don't know," Crockett said, his voice rueful. "Either you committed a crime or you didn't. Just reducing the charge doesn't make much sense. We need more facts. But what can I do?" He accepted the plea and put the youth on probation.

A tough-looking young white man, more than six feet tall and heavyset, came before Judge Crockett next. He was pleading guilty to attempted felonious assault.

"But it says here," Crockett interrupted, reading from the police report, "that you hit a man repeatedly with a beer bottle."

"It was just an argument," the defendant protested, and he described a sidewalk altercation in front of a barroom. First there were angry words, then he hit the other man with a beer bottle that he had carried out of the tavern with him. The victim was knocked to the ground.

"And then what happened?" Crockett asked.

"He got back up, so I hit him again," the man explained. "After a few more times, he didn't get up any more."

Crockett quieted loud laughter in the courtroom and stared straight ahead for a moment, seeming to search with anxious eyes for help in making sense of what he was hearing.

"And I understand that the victim nearly died," he said, more to himself than anyone else. "*Attempted* assault," he repeated, drawing out the word "attempted" very slowly. But Crockett had to accept the plea. He held the prosecutor's signed statement accepting it, sealing the bargain. There was no alternative. The system had decided.

The next defendant, a young black man in a blue suit

whose self-confident bearing was uncharacteristic for Recorders Court, told Crockett that he was a college student from Detroit attending school in Alabama, where he kept a gun to protect himself.

Driving back home with friends, he said, he had left the gun under the floor mat in the back seat of his car, where he had always kept it at school. As he drove through a white Detroit neighborhood, he recounted, his car was stopped by policemen, who said he was speeding but who gave him no ticket. Instead, they frisked him and his friends and searched the car, found the gun, and charged him with illegal possession of a concealed weapon.

In many ways, the student's case was similar to Sam Jackson's, except that this youngster had no prior police record. He was formally admitting guilt to the charge of not presenting the gun for registration.

Crockett appeared disturbed. "If the facts are what you say they are, you should not be pleading guilty," he told the youth. "Those policemen had no right to search you or your car—that is, *if* you are telling the truth. Without a trial, without questioning the policemen or other witnesses, I have no way of telling.

"That's what's wrong with this system." Crockett's voice rose. "If you're telling the truth, you shouldn't be convicted of anything. And what those police did should be brought out into the open. But, without a trial, I have no way of knowing if you're lying or not. This way, there is no review of this practice of police just pulling people over and going through their cars. That's why these things go on every day here, because we have vacated our responsibilities."

Always, in plea bargaining, compromises are struck between guilt and innocence. Little connection is made between what took place that led to the arrest of the accused, what happens to him in the courtroom, and what is done with him next. Decisions on putting a convicted man on probation or the length of his prison sentence are based most often on what must be done to seal a bargain for a guilty plea, rather than on whether or how a guilty person should be punished or rehabilitated. In fact, nobody can be certain that innocent persons are not being convicted or, more frequently, that habitual criminals are not being let off lightly. The first possibility undermines the very foundation of our legal system. The second increases daily disorder in society by reinforcing in the wrongdoer the belief that he need never really respect the law.

But plea bargaining is not the only shortcut to justice practiced regularly in criminal courts today. Many thousands of cases—in many places, half the court's serious criminal cases—never even get as far as the plea-bargaining stage. The defendants charged in them—innocent and guilty alike—are arbitrarily set free before a trial, in effect acquitted by default, because the overburdened system cannot accommodate them.

Under pressure to keep the judge's case calendar as light as possible, the prosecutor drops charges against defendants wholesale before the cases can reach the judge. These decisions, made by a young assistant prosecutor, usually overworked and inexperienced, are most often based on a quick glance at police reports of arrests. Summarily, he tosses out cases that seem too "weak"; cases involving charges, such as a husband's beating his wife, that seem too tawdry for the court to consider; those involving, as defendants, neat-looking, middle-class people who seem "respectable" and not likely to get into trouble again. Frequently, perhaps, the prosecutor is dispensing admirable justice and saving the system from needless further congestion. But nobody ever knows for sure. The prosecutor makes no investigation of his own before acting. Most often, no judge reviews his decision. Some judges, in their turn, throw out still more cases in large lots. The judges, too, base their decisions on no more than a look at a court paper or a remark from a prosecutor or defense lawyer.

Certain defendants, usually the often convicted and knowledgeable, win freedom simply by outwaiting the courts. Patiently, they endure delay after delay arising as a natural product of the overloaded system, and then they have their lawyers stall still longer with procedural tricks and requests for postponements that nobody has time to challenge. In the end, witnesses who have come back to court again and again stop showing up, or, as the months pass, even the most conscientious among them find their memories fading. Judges and prosecutors become impatient with musty cases that further bog down their operation, and a carefully timed request by the defense lawyer, often on a day when witnesses are not present, is enough to persuade a judge to throw the case out.

There still are trials. But, when a rare criminal trial does take place before a judge or a judge and jury, it is often a shadow drama of the real thing, played out by poorly prepared lawyers before obviously uninspired judges, who sometimes conduct their more productive guilty-plea business off to the side of the bench while the trial is in progress. Seldom, except for the most complicated, serious, or glamorous cases, has the prosecutor or even the defense lawyer —both of whom have crowded schedules of their own— planned what he was going to do in advance. Sometimes, the judge has to coach the prosecutor and defense lawyer to ask questions of witnesses or to make motions they would not otherwise have thought to make themselves. Or, conversely, the harried judge must work to speed up the case, reminding the lawyers not to "stall" with questions or arguments that seem to him unrewarding and prodding a jury that spends more than an hour or two deliberating its verdict. (Lawyers for both sides in the chaotic Manhattan

branch of New York City's Criminal Court say that a long
trial there is any that lasts more than ten minutes.)

In several cities, including Baltimore, Cleveland, and
Chicago, persons charged with misdemeanors—vagrancy,
disorderly conduct, simple assault, gambling, shoplifting,
and other petty thievery—are usually not represented by
lawyers when they are tried. In Baltimore's Municipal
Court, not even a prosecutor is present for criminal cases.
The arresting policeman, who often looks uncomfortable doing it, must present the government's evidence to the judge
and sometimes point out information favorable to the defendant that otherwise would be overlooked. The judge
must ask the questions that a prosecutor or defense lawyer
would ask, suggest the arguments, if any, that they might
make, and, in the end, decide the outcome of the case.
There is no jury, no court reporter, not even a court clerk.
Legal rules are treated nonchalantly, and such usually "in-
admissible" evidence as hearsay testimony often is allowed.

The assumption that anyone accused of a crime in the
United States has a right to a full adversary trial of his
guilt or innocence—with well-prepared advocates for each
side, carefully overseen by an able, even-handed judge,
searching diligently for the truth and satisfying all legal
rules and safeguards—is fundamental to the American system of justice and to the populace's confidence in it. Yet,
with few exceptions, this concept has become little more
than a still celebrated myth both in the folklore of the law
and in formal jurisprudence. Not only in Perry Mason
dramas, but also in real-life appellate court decisions, in the
body of criminal law, and in urgent legal controversies, the
myth is still believed to represent reality. As a result, there
exists little in the way of formal rules, high court pronouncements, or even informed legal or public opinion to
ensure that justice is done in the substitute way that men

and women are actually "tried" every day in American courts.

Instead, everything is left up to the criminal-court bureaucracy, which, like its counterparts throughout government and private commerce, is concerned first with its own day-to-day survival. Judge, prosecutor, defense attorney, policeman, and clerk are working partners struggling to keep their heads above water as the flood of cases rises. Is it not natural that, for them, expediency should take precedence over justice, eventually becoming one and the same with it in the minds of bureaucrats?

Only a few voices from within raise any alarm. A bar association in New York City condemns "mass assembly-line justice" that rushes defendants into guilty pleas "in violation of their legal rights." A New York State appellate judge warns that "instant justice" is "converting our courthouses into counting houses." An exasperated Washington, D.C., lawyer, now chief judge of the General Sessions court there, complains that criminal courts have become "factories where defendants are quickly processed like so many sausages."

"Wherever the visitor looks at the system, he finds great numbers of defendants being processed by harassed and overworked officials," the widely respected legal educator and researcher Edward L. Barrett, Jr., has stated. "Suddenly, it becomes clear that for most defendants in the criminal process, there is scant regard for them as individuals. They are numbers on dockets, faceless ones to be processed and sent on their way. The gap between theory and reality is enormous."

Indeed, momentous Supreme Court decisions and currently fashionable public and legal debates over criminal law and the rights of the accused are simply irrelevant to what actually happens each day inside the courtroom. In many cities, judges and lawyers never bother to explain to defendants (as appellate courts have instructed them to do) those various constitutional rights they can invoke to protect them in court. Despite high court rulings on the right to a lawyer, many defendants still do not have one, or else they wind up with courthouse hangers-on of dubious ability who can get no other clients. The admissibility at a trial of a confession obtained by police is perhaps the most debated public issue concerning criminal courts, but it is essentially a moot question in a system where 90 per cent of those convicted admit guilt, anyway, in the courtroom. Appellate court decisions and legal controversies over what evidence can be used against defendants when they are tried are virtually meaningless when few defendants are ever actually brought to trial. Accusations that judges are too lenient or too harsh on criminals, or too pro- or anti-police, assume powers that judges often no longer exercise in deciding guilt or innocence, or even fixing sentences, in many criminal cases.

Mass-production criminal justice in the United States dates back at least to before the first national surveys of American courts in the 1920's and 1930's began to document and decry the gradual disappearance of adversary justice in criminal courtrooms. (No systematic study has ever been made of the workings and consequences of the mass-production processes that have evolved, such as plea bargaining.) But expediency has not necessarily meant efficiency. In many cities, for example, the court system's traditional disorganization and the avalanche of work now crashing down onto it seem to be leading inevitably to the day when the criminal-court machinery may grind to a standstill.

"They are just spinning their wheels now," observes one veteran lawyer about the New York City criminal courts. As an official of the Vera Institute for Justice, a nonprofit legal-reform "think tank," he is studying and trying to devise change for the city's courts.

"People talk about the criminal courts breaking down," he says. "The fact is, here at least, they *have* broken down. But nobody wants to admit it."

The volume of criminal cases in New York City's court system has more than doubled in a decade, and each judge must face as many as 200 serious criminal cases each day. One of the most respected jurists on the bench of Criminal Court in Manhattan, Simon Silver, abruptly resigned in late 1969 because he was "fed up with congestion."

"I feel I cannot give the cases the real attention they're entitled to," Judge Silver said, when he decided to step down after twenty-two years' service as a magistrate and judge before his current term expired. "As each case comes up, a judge should have the time to listen to the lawyers, to evaluate the situation, to determine whether violence is involved and must seriously be considered. The defendant's background should be explored, and the reasons for his actions. Sudden emotional flare-ups should be treated differently from crimes that seem to be chronic.

"At present, I find that I cannot dispose satisfactorily of more than fifteen cases a day. The rest [usually 100 to 200 or more] are adjourned [postponed to another day], and that creates a heavier backlog. I have to spend more time on [postponements] than in listening, considering, and disposing."

Despite the haste with which many other criminal-court judges run through cases, there are, on any given day, more than 7,000 criminal defendants in jail awaiting their turn in New York City courts. One such lockup, adjacent to the Criminal Court Building in Manhattan and known appropriately as the Tombs, was built for 900 prisoners but has held as many as 2,000. Its population was near that number in August, 1970, when 300 angry prisoners took over one floor, held several guards hostage, and vandalized what they could—all to protest the jail's crowded conditions and the long pretrial delays. "The ironic thing," Commissioner of Corrections George McGrath told reporters, "is that most of what they say I have said many times over the past months. The institution is abominably overcrowded."

In Detroit, Cleveland, Chicago, and Washington, D.C., defendants often must wait a year or longer for their cases to be tried or otherwise concluded. In Lynn, Massachusetts, late in 1969, a man charged with armed robbery was finally ordered freed unconditionally after the state failed to try his case within the two-year limit set by the state constitution.

The criminal courts are the neglected stepchildren of already overcrowded, undermanned, niggardly financed, and hopelessly antiquated state and local systems of trial courts. In New York City, some criminal-court judges must conduct court in converted clerks' offices and judges' robing rooms. In Baltimore, Cleveland, and Chicago, among other places, most misdemeanor cases are tried in makeshift courtrooms located on the upper floors of old police station houses, while the police continue doing business downstairs. These rooms are like those in old tenements, with exposed pipes, peeling paint, falling plaster, and splintered wood. Only secondhand accessories and an old desk for the judge make them officially courtrooms. There is seldom room for half the participants to sit.

In Chicago, felony cases are tried in the deteriorating Cook County Criminal Court Building adjacent to the notoriously run-down county jail. Its badly lit, acoustically impossible, poorly maintained courtrooms provide a stark contrast to the bright, well-designed, extravagantly furnished modern courtrooms provided for the city's well-heeled civil-case lawyers and litigants in the new thirty-floor, glass-and-steel Civic Center downtown. In city after city, the criminal court is kept separate, in older buildings and rundown neighborhoods, from the rest of the trial courts and their silk-suited barristers who operate in the better downtown districts. Nowhere do the criminal courts have enough judges or supporting personnel. Methods for scheduling cases and keeping records, usually all done by hand, have remained largely unchanged since courts were first established in the American colonies.

Criminal court is where the chief judge sends rookie, hack, or senile judges who cannot be trusted with complicated civil cases. The majority of the private-practice lawyers appearing before them are counterparts of Detroit's Clinton Street bar (called "Fifth Streeters" in Washington, D.C., and the "Baxter Street bar" in New York City). They wait for judges to appoint them to cases, or they prowl the halls soliciting work from defendants and relatives of defendants who pass by. If they are not paid by the local or state government, management of their client's cases is built around efforts to extract money from defendants or relatives. The client is told bluntly that the quality of service depends on the fee. If time is needed for the money to be raised, the lawyer has the case postponed in court. Judges knowingly cooperate in this fee-collection effort by postponing the case without reason when a lawyer gives the signal. In New York, the attorney usually tells the judge he needs time to locate a witness, a "Mr. Green."

The derelicts who seek and often find peaceful repose on the front steps or inside the corridors of criminal court buildings in city after city make the message clear: Criminal court is for the dregs of society and the lowly of the legal community.

The absence of much concern, scrutiny, or help from the outside reinforces in criminal-court bureaucrats a profound cynicism and resistance to criticism and change. Eventually, the malaise overtakes even many of the young and idealistic newcomers joining the staffs of the prosecutor, public defender, or probation-office chief.

This "hostile attitude toward 'outsiders'" is actually a "defensiveness" on the part of courthouse bureaucrats, who must each day satisfy the demands of assembly-line disposal of intolerably large case loads by legal "shortcuts, deviations, and outright rule violations adopted as court practice," observes Abraham Blumberg, a noted lawyer and sociologist who has been studying mass-production justice from a new perspective. "Fearfully anticipating criticism on ethical as well as legal grounds," participants in the court's social structure are "bound into an organized system of complicity," Blumberg has written in his book *Criminal Justice* based on a study of big-city criminal courts. "Breaches and invasions of 'due process' are institutionalized, but are, nevertheless, denied to exist.

"Accused persons come and go in the court system," Blumberg points out, "but the structure and its personnel remain." To keep going, to survive the pressures of the work load, and to avoid facing the injustices they are party to,

> they must preserve their own relations and interaction at all costs.
>
> The client becomes a secondary figure in the court system. He may present doubts, contingencies, and pressures which challenge or disrupt . . . but they are usually resolved in favor of the organization. Even the accused's lawyer has far greater professional, economic, and other ties to the various elements of the court system than to his own client. In short, the court is a closed community.

Nowhere is Blumberg's analysis better documented than in New York City's Criminal Court in lower Manhattan. There, in the dingy, tomblike building teeming daily with people, can be found typical, if sometimes extreme, examples of the distortions of justice that assembly-line processing produces at every stage in the criminal-court system.

The nerve center of Criminal Court is Part 1-A. Through it, during daytime and evening sessions, passes a daily procession of 200 to 500 defendants arrested that day or the night before for every kind of crime. Most are represented at this initial hearing by lawyers from the Legal Aid Society, a quasi-public defender supported by the city and private donors. Those who can afford it hire their own lawyers—frequently from the Baxter Street bar—before their next date in court, if there is one.

The pandemonium in Part 1-A is unique even for a criminal court. Defendants on bail, victims of and witnesses to crimes, and others crowd the wooden benches and line the walls. Dozens of police in street clothes, with badges pinned on suits, sport shirts, and windbreakers, scurry about, retrieving defendants for their cases from the public pews or the lockup behind the court, bringing them and their papers before the judge, and returning them after each case. The scene in front of the judge is a constant jumble of people bumping into one another, as defendants, policemen, and witnesses for each case come and go. The pace is so rapid that the judge himself often has time only to check his calendar and set dates for cases to be continued to another day. Most of the talking is done by a bailiff called the "bridgeman," who, in each courtroom of Manhattan's Criminal Court, stands just below the judge on the bottom level of the two-tiered platform.

"Numbers 104, 105, 106, 107, 108, and 109, step up here," a swarthy, dark-haired, gruff-voiced bridgeman shouts, in calling a case with six defendants arrested for possession of narcotics. "Hurry it up. Hurry it up."

The defendants squeeze between the prosecutor and the Legal Aid lawyer in front of the judge. Policemen and witnesses crowd around them. The two lawyers operate in shifts with other prosecutors and defenders. Each stands for about an hour in front of the judge, taking cases as they come. The prosecutor knows nothing about a case until it is called and he sees the court papers on it for the first time. Sometimes, the Legal Aid lawyer has interviewed defendants briefly through the bars in the lockup, or he is given a scanty fact sheet by another defender who saw the prisoner.

In a tobacco-auctioneer's rapid, singsong style, the bridgeman reads the formal charge against the defendants so fast it can barely be understood.

"Put up your hands," the bridgeman orders the policemen who made the arrest. Under New York law, they must swear to the veracity of the charge they filed. They stick up their right hands, but they are not really paying attention to the bridgeman; they are explaining their case in whispers to the prosecutor. The Legal Aid lawyer leans over to try to overhear them. The bridgeman rattles off the oath "Officers, do-you-swear-that-this-is-the-affidavit-you-signed?" No response, but it doesn't matter. "Put your hands down," the bridgeman growls.

"All right, QUIET in here," he interrupts himself to shout. "Shut that door back there."

"Howdya plead? howdya plead?" the bridgeman demanded of the Legal Aid attorney, a young blonde woman, on one typical day. She asked a few whispered questions of some of the defendants and turned to the prosecutor to confer with him.

"Let's go. "Let's go," the bridgeman barked. "Officers, number 110, Stanton is next. Have the prisoner ready. We've got to move along."

After a few more words with the Legal Aid lawyer, the prosecutor announced that charges against four of the men would be dropped. There was no explanation why. A date was set for the trial of the other two, who pleaded not guilty.

"All right, all right, you can go," the bridgeman told the four who were let go. "Hurry it up."

The other two men were returned to the lockup, but the bridgeman first had to advise them of their rights. This is his most practiced speech, a series of rapid sentences, each recited as if it were one word and delivered without looking up as he sifts through his papers for the next case: "You-understand-you-have-the-right-to-an-attorney-or-the-right-to-an-adjournment-to-procure-the-services-of-one. If-you-do-not-have-the-financial-resources-to-afford-an-attorney-the-court-will-appoint-one-for-you. You-also-have-the-right-to-communicate-free-of-charge-by-telephone-or-mail-with-any-officer-of-the-court."

His voice rose, "All right, put the prisoners away. Take them away."

Already, he was calling the next case. "Number 110. Stanton. Let's go. Step to the other side of your attorney, mister. Hands out of your pockets. Officer, put your hand up."

Frequently, defendants and witnesses are rushed away by the bridgeman before they understand what has been decided about the case or when and where they are to return to court for the next hearing. In many cases, nothing more is done than the setting of a date for trial. Other cases are dismissed by the prosecutor, usually with no reason given. Occasionally, a guilty plea is arranged on the spot after a whispered conference in front of the judge. The judge passes sentence right away.

In one case, the Legal Aid lawyer announced that her client wanted to plead guilty to assaulting a policeman. But the defendant said he "didn't hit nobody." The judge ordered a date set for trial.

No case lasts more than five minutes. Many are over in sixty seconds.

During a break, one young prosecutor just out of law school said he likes the system. "It becomes routine," he explained with some pride. "You can look at the first couple of lines on the [police] complaint and tell what the case is about, what the state can prove. The defense attorney is equally skilled. You just learn to think quickly on your feet. It's fascinating. I enjoy it."

Nearly 300 cases were being processed in Part 1-A on October 14, 1970, when Julio Roldan, thirty-four years old—a high-strung Puerto Rican poet, seller of handicrafts, and new member of the Young Lords, the radical Puerto Rican political party in New York—was brought before the judge on a charge of arson growing out of a Young Lords street protest the night before. The protest was over poor garbage collection. In vain, Roldan had complained to the arresting policemen that he and a friend were only trying to stamp out garbage set on fire on the sidewalk by someone else.

After waiting in jail overnight, and in the courthouse lockup from 7:30 A.M., Roldan came before the judge for his brief arraignment at 2:30 P.M. The prosecutor had already processed thirty new cases during the hour following the lunch break. He had not seen the papers on Roldan before 2:30, when, glancing at the information placed before him—including the fact that Roldan was a Young Lord, an identification that frequently draws a hostile reaction from law enforcement agents in New York—he recommended that $2,500 bail bond be set. Roldan's lawyer was in court, but he had not been given an opportunity to interview his client in the lockup during the long wait before arraignment. He protested and asked that Roldan be freed without bond or at least have the opportunity to confer with him first. Roldan himself, obviously upset, cried out, "There is no justice in this court. There is no one here to represent us. This is only happening because I am Puerto Rican."

The judge, pointing out that he was swamped with business, granted a delay, and the lawyer, who did volunteer work for the Young Lords but had not met Roldan previously, began to argue that his client's emotional condition suggested he should be sent to a hospital for observation. Before the lawyer could argue further, as a transcript of the proceedings later showed, the judge cut him off in midsentence and set bail at $1,500. There was no more time to waste on this case, the judge told the lawyer. "We are working under adverse conditions . . . I can't create the Utopia here."

Roldan did not have the bail money or the premium payment of more than $100 that was required to obtain a bail bond in that large an amount. He was sent next door to the towering Tombs jail and there put in an 8-by-8-by-6-foot all-steel cell. During the next two days, Julio Roldan apparently grew increasingly irrational. On the third morning of his confinement, guards coming by to count prisoners at 8:30 A.M. found him dead, hanging by his belt from a steel bar in the rear of his cell.

"Ordinarily, in view of his outbursts in court, he would have been assigned to an observation cell used to keep potential suicides under surveillance," according to a detailed report from the city's corrections department made later to Mayor John V. Lindsay. "However, word of his outbursts did not reach jail officials, so he was treated as a routine case."

Roldan's suicide briefly became a *cause célèbre* in New York City. The report the mayor ordered on the incident offered a rare glimpse into the horror of both the Tombs and the criminal court. On the day Roldan was arraigned, the report showed, the criminal-court judge devoted an average of only 102 seconds to each case that came up before him.

"The courtroom is crowded and noisy," the report said. "The judges who preside are themselves offended by the lack of decorum and the practical necessity of moving the calendar of cases."

In the letter transmitting the "Report to the Mayor of New York on the Death of a Citizen, Julio Roldan," the city's corrections board chairman, William J. vanden Heuvel, concluded,

> Julio Roldan died by his own hand on Oct. 16, 1970. But the intricate system of criminal justice which we have designed to protect the community and the individual succeeded only in deranging him and ultimately, instead of protecting him, it permitted his destruction.

From Part 1-A, cases go to myriad other branches, depending on the nature of the charge, supposedly to be tried. But most of the branches are mere clerking operations in which dates are set by the judges for further postponements of the cases. The prosecutor is waiting for the defendant to agree to plead guilty. The defendant is trying to outwait the government and have the case dismissed. The excuses for delays run the gamut, but nobody believes them or cares. By court rule, after several postponements, the judge marks the next excuse the "final" one for the defendant or the government. But that means nothing. Cases wind up marked "final, final, final" against the defendant or government, and yet more postponements are granted. Witnesses, told they must show up each time the case is scheduled, are forced to return to court five and six times on the average, often only to find the case dismissed or the defendant pleading guilty. Only 5 per cent of all cases are eventually tried by a judge. "If even 10 per cent ended in a trial," one prosecutor says, "the system would break down."

The judge's main function in courtroom after courtroom is merely to consult a calendar and order "Pick a date" for each case to be postponed to. Baxter Street lawyers seem to limit their practice to asking judges for delays and pleading their clients guilty. They buttonhole new prospects in the halls and confer with current clients in the aisles of courtrooms even as judges are conducting business.

Occasionally, a trial is held. Most defendants in trials are represented by Legal Aid lawyers. Often, the defender and the prosecutor are friends and carry on playful banter during the brief trial. To save time, they make agreements on many issues beforehand. Their case presentations are austere.

In one such trial, a middle-aged Puerto Rican man, with a wife and two children, was charged with indecent exposure at a subway station. The complaining witness was a secretary whom he had annoyed. The prosecutor, a pretty young woman with long brown hair, could not resist smiling and joking with "Bill," the Legal Aid lawyer, during the fifteen-minute trial. The case was already a year old and had been postponed nine times. Both the defendant and the secretary were tense and confused as they tried to recall the incident. The prosecutor cleverly trapped the defendant into making an error in his story. The judge was persuaded and found the man guilty.

"Your talents were wasted on that one, Bill," the prosecutor told the Legal Aid lawyer as the case ended.

"I tried to get him to plead guilty to loitering months ago," Bill explained. "But he wouldn't do it."

The same rush to dispose of cases—the same lack of concern for criminal defendants as individual human beings—carries over to the final important step in criminal courts: sentencing convicted defendants. Little effort is made to connect the background of a convict and the nature of his offense with the decision of what to do with him next—a decision that not only profoundly shapes the rest of his life but also affects public safety. It is much less often a reasoned decision than it is the foregone conclusion of a bargain for a guilty plea, the end product of an inflexible law, the product of the prejudices of a particular judge, or the result of a hurried moment in a crowded courtroom.

Usually, the prosecutor and defense lawyer have already

agreed on a certain sentence in exchange for a guilty plea. In addition, the sentence for a particular charge often is dictated by state law, and thus it is the charge itself for which a guilty-plea bargain has been struck. There are wide differences from state to state in the penalties set by law for various crimes. The minimum sentence for burglary is, in eight states, one year in prison, two to ten years in many others, and a life sentence in one. Sentences for rape vary from one year in prison to the death penalty. In some jurisdictions, judges are forbidden to grant probation to defendants convicted of certain crimes. California is one of the few states in which a judge is given wide latitude by the law to decide for himself what sentence to hand down.

But, even when not prevented by law or a prosecutor's deal from tailoring his sentence to each convict's particular case, many judges decide on sentences that make little sense and result in obvious inequities. A study of 800 cases in Detroit's Recorders Courts showed that black defendants and those wearing work clothes received much harsher sentences on the average than did whites and those wearing coats and ties who were convicted of the same crimes. The most severe Recorders Court judge sent nine of every ten defendants to prison; the most lenient jailed fewer than four of ten.

Court-wise defendants find ways to have their cases postponed, of course, until they come before a lenient judge—a common practice in criminal courts that is known as "judge shopping." In Manhattan, the same judge who let off with a fine a convicted stockbroker, who had realized $20 million in illegal trading, then turned around and sentenced a black, unemployed shipping clerk to a year in prison for stealing a $100 television set from a truck shipment.

"If you had pleaded guilty to this offense, I might have been more lenient with you," a Washington, D.C., judge recently told a young defendant whom he had sentenced to the legal maximum of five to fifteen years in prison. The youth had been convicted, at age eighteen, of holding up a bus driver with a toy pistol. The judge made it clear at the hearing for sentencing that he was displeased that the youth had persisted in claiming his innocence while on the witness stand during his trial and again before the judge after his conviction, despite the "evidence being overwhelming as it was." The judge said he would be more lenient when a defendant told him, "Judge, I am sorry for what I did."

In his celebrated book *The Crime of Punishment*, Dr. Karl Menninger, the noted psychiatrist and penal reformer, writes that "all humans have some share in the impulse to violence, that people subconsciously want crime, gain satisfaction from inadequate handling of it, gain satisfaction from the infliction of pain on the criminal."

Citing that argument, a California judge said, "We judges share these human impulses. Some crimes are so repellent, so hideously excessive, that the perpetrator arouses anger and disgust. Who has not felt an impulse to throttle the brutish Neanderthal whose offense surpasses all understanding? Judges are not exempt from hatred, not immune from the temptation to swing mankind's avenging sword."

The vengeance wrought against criminals in the United States shocks people in other countries. Prison sentences for most crimes average many years longer in the United States than in other politically stable nations. A committee of the American Bar Association that studied the sentencing process concluded that "sentences are in most cases much higher than is usually called for by the particular offense." The committee recommended that most sentences for serious crimes, which frequently run to ten, twenty, or more years' maximum imprisonment, "be sharply reduced to approximately the five year range," except for demonstrably uncontrollable offenders.

The sentencing function in American criminal courts lies outside much of the supposed due-process system, has little appellate review, is often performed on the basis of very few facts and sometimes on the basis of much misinformation, and depends on capricious or prejudiced snap judgments by those involved. Facts concerning the identity of each defendant, his background, the crime he committed, and the prospects of his rehabilitation seldom come to light. In the majority of the nation's criminal-court cases, sentence is passed by a judge who has no more information than a few hasty comments made by the prosecutor and defense attorney—or by the defendant himself if he has no lawyer.

In many large criminal courts, judges are supplied with "presentence" reports on some or all of the defendants, which are supposed to present a complete picture of the defendant: his family life, schooling, job history, mental and physical health, and previous criminal record. If the defendant has pleaded guilty—as nine out of ten do—the presentence report also supplies the judge with the only official account of the crime for which the defendant was convicted. In many jurisdictions, the report also contains a recommendation for sentencing by the person who prepared the report—usually, the court probation officer.

The problem is that, like everyone else in the system, probation officers are overworked and undersupervised. Consequently, many presentence reports amount to little more than recitations of the police or prosecutor's version of the crime, the defendant's past police record, dates concerning his birth, schooling, and employment, and the probation officer's impressions written after a brief interview with the defendant. Stray derogatory remarks by policemen or prosecutors, which would never be admitted in open court, often find their way into the hastily written reports, as do outright errors and large doses of the writer's prejudices as stimulated by the defendant's life style or the alleged crime. Many probation officers automatically recommend harsh sentences for a defendant with a history of hard drinking or deviant sexual practices or who seems aggressive or unrepentant during his brief interview.

Seldom are defendants tested psychologically. Seldom are their relatives, employers, or friends interviewed. Seldom is the defendant questioned sufficiently to reveal much about him.

In a highly unusual appellate ruling in 1962, the New Jersey Superior Court (in *State* v. *Leckis*) strongly criticized a typical presentence report that presented only the police version of the crime, a felonious assault plus

> a repetition of the defendant's previous record, a very brief family history limited to names, ages, religion and residence of his mother, father and sister, his claim that he was never married, the fact that defendant attended school only through the eighth grade, his employment record, army record, religion and a notation that in his leisure time he admits to drinking too much. . . .
>
> There is little in the report that would give a judge an accurate idea of the defendant's personal background—his mentality, personality, habits, and the like—or of the family background which would give the case meaningful setting. . . .
>
> We find strong indications in the record suggesting that if defendant had been fairly interviewed by a probation department representative in whom he had some confidence, and the entire background of the occurrence disclosed, the degree of his offense might well have been tempered and his punishment proportionately lightened. So much depends upon the completeness and balanced presentation of a presentence report that anything less would fall short of providing the sentencing judge with the information he must have in order to impose a just sentence.

In most jurisdictions, the defendant and his lawyer are not allowed to see the presentence report and are therefore unable to present evidence to counter bias or incomplete information. Defendants are not even guaranteed the right to be represented by a lawyer at sentencing. Lawyers who are present seldom take the trouble to make a presentence investigation of their own or to contact the court employees who prepare the one used by the judge. Appellate courts usually do not review criminal sentences or the sentencing process, no matter how bizarre or unjust a case may be.

Avoiding "unnecessary" trials, processing the sausages with the bridgeman's unremitting haste, ignoring the fates of defendants and crime victims alike, blotting them out as human beings—this, in sum, is the business of criminal courts across the country. The necessity to move cases quickly is the central need. Determining guilt or innocence, deciding on the treatment of offenders, and dealing with those in the public who are dragged into the process are all secondary matters. Means are shaped not in accordance with the constitutional ideal of justice but, rather, to satisfy the ends of the bureaucracy in its daily battle with case loads.

Plea bargaining was given the stamp of high court approval in April, 1970, when the U.S. Circuit Court of Appeals in New York upheld the conviction of a man who claimed he had pleaded guilty to a second-degree murder charge only because he was told he would be prosecuted for first-degree murder, and possibly executed, if he insisted on a trial. Then, in late 1970, the U.S. Supreme Court also upheld a guilty plea made for the same reason. Its narrow ruling, which left unanswered the broader legal questions about the propriety of plea bargaining as it is conducted in most cases in the lower courts, was that a man can knowingly decide to plead guilty only to avoid the possibility of the death penalty rather than because he philosophically admits his guilt, and that he cannot change his mind later.

The New York federal appellate court ruling went further, in that it took pains to sanction plea bargaining generally as an alternative to the chaos that it believed might result if plea bargaining ceased and all those criminal defendants who now plead guilty (ninety-five of every hundred New York "convictions") had to be given trials instead. Without plea bargaining, "the administration of criminal justice as we know it would be impossible," Chief Judge Edward Lumbard wrote for the unanimous three-judge panel in New York. Such a judgment elevates the courthouse bureaucracy's substitution of expediency for justice to a lofty level of respectability.

A committee of the American Bar Association, concerned with minimum standards for criminal justice, has declared that "conviction without trial will and should continue to be a more frequent means for the disposition of criminal cases." The system "cannot operate effectively unless trial judges in fact grant charge and sentence concessions to most defendants who enter a plea of guilty."

This is one of the committee's conclusions in a recent report on plea bargaining made without a controlled study of the process—and presented despite the fact that, later in the same report, the committee virtually contradicts itself by insisting that judges should still consider "rehabilitative, protective, or deterrent" purposes in passing sentence, and should not impose heavier than justified sentences whenever "the defendant has chosen to require the prosecution to prove his guilt at trial."

The Republic has not been consulted. The Constitution has not been amended. But someone has here adopted a different standard for justice than the one that has always been a first lesson in civics for school children. Imagine a defendant *requiring* the government to prove his guilt at trial.

What can one conclude but that David Burnham, the award-winning crime reporter for the *New York Times*, was right in his disgusted reaction to what is happening today in criminal courts? In describing Manhattan's Criminal Court as "the most cynical place in the world," he in effect described every other criminal court in the United States.

III

The Revolving-Door Problems

One step inside "drunk court" in Cleveland, Ohio, the stench of stale whisky, urine, sweat, and vomit confronts the visitor. Sitting down and staying put on one of the dusty old wood benches in the small, stifling courtroom, on the second floor of police headquarters, becomes a test of endurance for mind and stomach.

In the dim light, dozens of haggard men in tattered clothing stand in a seemingly endless line that stretches along a peeling green wall on the side of the courtroom, through a door behind the judge, down a hall leading from a hidden cellblock. These men are alcoholics, arrested the night before for public drunkenness. Most are middle-aged, but they look older, their bodies emaciated, their skin pallid. Some cough and retch violently. A few, suffering delirium tremens, shake uncontrollably, as though they were freezing cold in the hot, sticky courtroom.

These diseased men will find no help in this stinking, depressing place. Many are simply released by the judge to go back to the streets. Others may be sent to jail for a few days, weeks, or months. But it is a safe bet that most of them will return sooner or later to Cleveland's drunk court. They are addicted to alcohol, and nothing is done in the court system or the jail to treat their condition.

With very few exceptions, criminal courts throughout the United States handle alcoholics just as Cleveland's does. These courts are revolving doors through which alcoholics go from bottle to court, perhaps to jail, and back to the bottle again, untouched by their brief contact with criminal justice.

Tragically, drunk court is not the only revolving door in America's criminal courts. Through others pass narcotics addicts, gamblers, prostitutes, vagrants, abortionists, homosexuals, and persons arrested for adulterous or "unnatural" sex acts. Because the law has singled out these people as criminals, the courts are expected to stop their deviant behavior. But, in every case, the goal is unrealistic if not impossible as a practical matter and illogical if not unreasonable in moral terms.

Narcotics addicts, for instance, suffer just as alcoholics do from a physical or psychological illness that the criminal-court process simply does not treat. Women who desperately want to abort their pregnancies will find a way to do it no matter what the law says or the courts do. Gamblers and adulterous couples see no reason why their conduct should be illegal, and they are supported in that belief by the actions if not the words of a majority of citizens. Vagrants do not suddenly find steady jobs, rented rooms, or respectability after being taken before a judge. Homosexuals cannot be converted to heterosexuality by the courts. In short, few if any of these kinds of defendants can be expected to change their ways after being processed through the criminal courts. Nor should they be expected to.

Still more important to our ideal of justice is the fact that these people, labeled as "criminals," are not maliciously threatening the persons or property of other citizens when engaging in the behavior prohibited by law. Some of them —narcotics addicts, for example—may be endangering themselves, or their actions may be repugnant to other citizens.

But, in their cases, the criminal law and courts are being used solely to dictate personal morality or control real or imagined self-abuse, rather than for their legitimate (but overstretched) purpose of prohibiting one citizen from harming another.

When harm is done, it turns out that the law and the courts themselves are sometimes the agents of destruction—forcing addicts to steal to pay inflated black market prices for heroin, pushing gamblers and prostitutes under the umbrella of organized crime, delivering women seeking abortion into the hands of renegade or amateur physicians working in unsanitary surroundings, and making possible the humiliation, persecution, and even imprisonment of harmless, otherwise law-abiding citizens whose private sexual proclivities happen to differ from society's assumed norms. These are human crimes committed under laws that are supposed to control crime, and by courts that are supposed to work justice.

Law sociologist Herbert Packer, among other experts, argues, in his book *The Limits of the Criminal Sanction*, that in all these instances the criminal sanction has been "misplaced." Treating these activities or social conditions as crimes is, in many cases, unnecessary interference in private conduct or, in other cases, a mistaken and dangerously ineffective way to deal with very real social problems. Packer and several other legal writers have recently begun to urge that this "overreaching" of the criminal law be stopped and that these cases be removed from the criminal courts.

Even the influential President's Commission on Law Enforcement and the Administration of Justice (popularly known as the "Crime Commission"), a mid-1960's panel strongly oriented toward traditional law enforcement views, called for study of the "problem of over-reliance upon the criminal law as a means of social regulation [in] instances in which the use of the penalties and processes of the criminal law have proven particularly ineffective or costly or both." The Commission carefully concluded, "It would seem . . . that civil processes or institutions designed to handle particular social problems would be more effective than the criminal process in many cases."

For chronic alcoholics, for instance, the Crime Commission said, the "search for alternatives is imperative." As it pointed out, there are now over 2 million drunkenness arrests in the United States every year. The parade of hopeless alcoholics through drunk court each day provides a vivid, recurring drama of the inhumane absurdity that results from misapplication of the criminal sanction.

In Cleveland's drunk court, the judge and uniformed policemen serving as bailiffs appear untouched by the misery of the wretched men lined up along the green wall. One by one, the men are sent staggering before the judge. On a day in the spring of 1970, the presiding judge appeared to recognize at least every other face.

"You again?" he inquired mockingly of one rubber-kneed man. "Go on home. One night in jail is enough."

Others, for one reason or another, were sent back to jail.

"You were here Monday, and you're back again?" the judge asked another derelict. "Thirty days in the work-house."

A policeman-bailiff wrote the number "30" on a scrap of paper and pressed it into the hand of the defendant, who was pointed back toward the cellblock.

"You've been here as many times as there are stops on the Broadway bus line," the judge told another defendant and then laughed loudly at his own joke.

"I don't drink much, your honor."

Another laugh, "You live on Buckeye, and you don't drink

much?" the judge said, referring to a street in a rough-and-tumble ethnic neighborhood on Cleveland's east side. "I'm afraid that I'll have to give you fifteen days."

Another defendant said he was from out of town and intended to leave Cleveland. "You're on your way now," the judge told him. "Hurry it up."

The judge remembered that yet another defendant had promised to return to Detroit after he was last brought to court for drunkenness a week earlier. "Maybe thirty days in jail will refresh your memory," the judge said. "Take him away."

Drunk court, for all practical purposes, is a court without trials. As each defendant was brought before the judge, he was told by the bailiff, "You're charged with intoxication. How do you plead?"

Usually, the answer was either "guilty" or a mumbled explanation or both. But it really did not matter. Each man had obviously been drinking to excess. Most turned up periodically in drunk court. Their guilt or innocence was not really at issue.

In drunk court in San Francisco, the scene is much the same, except that the drunkenness defendants are usually "tried" twenty or more at a time by the bailiff, who asks each large group, "Do any of you plead not guilty?"

Almost always, none does. "All guilty, your honor," the bailiff reports as he turns back to the judge, who then sentences the men individually.

"You don't look so good," the judge in San Francisco told one defendant. "I think we better take care of you. Thirty days in jail would do you good. Thirty days."

In cities with severe winters, drunk-court judges often sentence their regular customers to ninety or 120 days in jail during winter months to provide them, the judges say, with warm meals and shelter.

Drunk court in Detroit is used, as are drunk courts in

many cities, to collect fines. If the alcoholic cannot pay, he is sent to jail. On one ordinary day in Detroit's drunk court, a man given the standard sentence of "$25 or 30 days" told the judge he had only $16 in his pocket.

"I'll take the $16," the judge said. Amid laughter in the courtroom, he added, "Sometimes, justice works in mysterious ways."

A mystery, perhaps, but hardly justice. The revolving door of the criminal-court process does nothing to treat the disease of chronic alcoholism or to rehabilitate the alcoholic himself. It is only a matter of time before he returns to drunk court after being rearrested while lying on the sidewalk or on a park bench or hustling passers-by for the price of another pint of cheap whisky or wine. "Sending them to jail," Packer writes, "serves only the dubious social purpose of getting alcoholics out of sight for a while."

One city, Saint Louis, has made a concentrated effort to interrupt the revolving-door cycle by ceasing to haul drunks into court. They are taken instead to hospitals for twenty hours of medically supervised "drying out." Alcoholics with other medical problems or those who want to help in fighting their disease are hospitalized for longer periods. In Washington, D.C., after the U.S. Court of Appeals for the District of Columbia ruled that chronic alcoholism was a sickness rather than a crime, defendants, when judged in court to be chronic alcoholics, began to be sent to special in-patient treatment centers. But, in both cities, the projects have fallen far short of being cure-alls for alcoholism. Too little money is spent on long-term care and therapy, and the treatment period is too short, forcing uncured alcoholics back onto the streets. (In Washington, D.C., many downtown parks now have heroic statuary, Lady Bird Johnson's splendid plantings, and their own regulars among the city's drunks to offer as tourist attractions.) In addition, medical knowledge of alcoholism, its causes, and possible cures is still very limited, and there are also serious legal problems in compelling anyone to undergo treatment if he does not want it. However, the alcoholics of Saint Louis and Washington are being treated no worse and likely somewhat more beneficially than they were in the criminal-court process. At the same time, the two cities have removed thousands of pointless drunkenness cases each year from their overloaded court dockets.

Alone among American cities, these two have made the only meaningful efforts to interrupt the turning of the revolving door for alcoholics. Elsewhere, there has been neglect or even resistance to some opportunities for reform. Despite a Fourth Circuit Court of Appeals ruling in 1966 that a chronic alcoholic (exemplified in this case by a man arrested more than 200 times for drunkenness) could no longer be tried as a criminal, the local courts in that federal appellate jurisdiction—Maryland, Virginia, and the Carolinas —continue to process alcoholics as they had before. For the majority of the nation's tens of thousands of chronic alcoholics, there is no treatment of their sickness, only further degradation as common criminals.

For the nation's burgeoning number of narcotics addicts —who can only illegally buy, possess, or use the substances that their bodies insatiably crave—the pattern is the same, except for an added, devastating twist. They must further break the law by stealing to pay black market prices for narcotics. Not only do they suffer themselves, but they are also driven to inflict suffering on others.

"By defining him as a criminal, we have pushed the addict in the direction of becoming one," argues noted criminologist Edwin M. Schur, sociology chairman at Tufts University, in *Our Criminal Society: The Social and Legal Sources of Crime in America*. "The human and social costs of this decision have been almost incalculable."

A gigantic law enforcement apparatus, fueled by boundless government appropriations that could have been used alternatively to support an extensive program of medical research and treatment of addiction, has succeeded only in concentrating a limited supply of narcotics into the hands of organized criminals. The demand continues to grow unabated; consequently, black-market prices continue to climb. Addicts, often created by other addict-pushers seeking new buyers to help finance their own habits, steal more and more. The result is that, far from controlling the use of narcotics, the criminal law, the law enforcement agents, and the courts have contributed to the growth of what may be the nation's most potent and pervasive source of crime: heroin addiction.

Heroin, once dispensed legally as a sedative, is really a depressant that slows down the user's world, creating a lazy euphoria or half-sleep that addicts call "nodding." The "high" of heroin is the pleasurable calmness, the escape from the tension (and often what seems to the user the hopelessness) of reality. As psychological and physical dependence overtakes the user and makes him an addict, he soon lives for highs alone. Nothing else—food, sex, or other human beings—interests him. The heroin addict's preoccupation with his narcotic leads to malnutrition, withdrawal from normal life functions, and various forms of mental illness. An abrupt interruption in regular dosage brings a withdrawal reaction that can cause severe nausea, cramps, and shock. Still more threatening is overdosage, usually caused by an occasional very pure quantity of heroin taken unknowingly by an addict who has become accustomed to the heavily diluted product of the black market. The physical shock is often so great that it causes death.

An acute heroin habit costs the addict each day between $50 and $100 and often more. To afford it, he must amass stolen goods worth from three to ten times the amount of money he receives after selling them to a "fence." Otherwise, he must steal cash, as more and more addicts are doing. The best estimates put the number of addicts in the United States in the hundreds of thousands. That means that the cost of their collective habits totals billions of dollars each year, most of which must be stolen.

From New York City, where the threat of burglary is the preoccupation of almost every apartment dweller, to Washington, D.C., where public fear of armed holdups by teen-aged addicts approaches hysteria, to Detroit, Chicago, and Los Angeles, society's failure to deal effectively with heroin addiction has made the drug public enemy number one.

But many people still are not convinced. They think of rising crime as a "law and order" problem of increasingly loose morality and lax courts. Only now are they being told by a few outspoken experts and public officials that more and more of the criminal defendants coming through the courts are heroin addicts, who steal because they must and who will go on stealing no matter what happens to them in court.

Judge Alfred Burka of the Court of General Sessions in Washington, D.C., where, in the early 1960's, few citizens worried about heroin addiction, says that in 1970 three of every four felony defendants who come before him are addicts. Some, he adds, are experiencing withdrawal symptoms in the courtroom. Again and again, during this author's tour of the criminal courts in the nation's largest cities, the judge's observations were borne out. Defendants standing trial for robbery, burglary, and other crimes openly admitted they were addicts. Others were betrayed by heavy eyelids, glazed eyes, or the nervousness that marks the early stages of withdrawal.

Urinalysis tests administered to all arrivals at the District of Columbia jail in August, 1969, showed that half had been using heroin just prior to being incarcerated. On the average, each had three previous convictions and had been arrested more often than that. In a 1966 survey of prisoners in New York City's huge corrections system, 40 per cent (nearly 10,000) of the inmates admitted to having used heroin before their arrests. New York is also where 224 teen-agers, with and without criminal records, died of heroin overdoses in 1969.

Often, heroin addiction is a fact of life inside prison walls, too. In the District of Columbia, an undercover investigation recently disclosed that half of the 600 inmates of the reformatory for felons were buying heroin smuggled in by prison employees and visitors. Similar discoveries of heavy clandestine narcotics traffic have been made in the state prisons of Ohio and Maryland, and the Cook County jail, among others. Some addicts claim they first became "hooked" on heroin while behind bars.

Even if he is successfully cut off from narcotics while in prison, and forced to undergo withdrawal "cold turkey," without the aid of treatment, the addict finds it nearly impossible to resist returning to drugs once he is back outside. "Upon release," Judge Burka says, "the addict is thrust back into his usual haunts and can obtain narcotics within hours. At the moment, there exists only a vicious cycle for the narcotic addict. There is no escape for him."

"Whatever impact the law enforcement effort does have is felt most strongly not by the big-time narcotics profiteer," Schur points out, "but by the addict himself." Another observer, Alfred Lindesmith, has lamented the "long, shabby, pitiful parade of indigent drug users . . . mostly Negroes" in the nation's criminal courts, not unlike the long lines of emaciated men in drunk court. In Chicago, in fact, drunk court is matched in atmosphere and misery by a "narcotics court" located alongside it in the police headquarters building.

Like chronic alcoholics, addicts often are arrested dozens of times each: for possession of narcotics or such "paraphernalia" as the syringes, "cookers," and needles used to handle

it, for selling narcotics, for prostitution, shoplifting, burglary, robbery, or, after compiling a long record, for "narcotic vagrancy," the charge used against those suspected of
being addicts with no legal means of support. One thirty-
nine-year-old Washington, D.C., black woman who now
lectures to suburban groups on the evils of narcotics addiction was herself arrested sixty-nine times and sent to prison
on fourteen occasions.

"A clearer case of misapplication of the criminal sanction
would be difficult to imagine," Packer argues. Despite or
because of the law and the courts, he points out, "we are
very far indeed from having eradicated heroin addiction."
Not only has the law enforcement effort failed, he adds, but
it has diverted attention and money from research into the
causes, effects, and cures of narcotics addiction. Packer ac-
cuses the "large and well-entrenched enforcement bureaucracy" of having "developed a vested interest in the *status
quo.*" It has succeeded, he says, in "thwarting" efforts to
reform narcotics laws and in "intimidating" doctors into
"neglecting" their responsibility to push for medical treatment of addicts—even with continued narcotics dosage, if
that is the only way at present.

The sole attempt at change that the law enforcement
bureaucracy has fostered is the practice of "civil commitment" in lieu of criminal prosecution of some addicts, which
is done in California and New York, and in the federal courts
for violation of federal narcotics laws. Judges in these jurisdictions can order an addict to be sent to a hospital facility
for what is supposed to be treatment, while his court case
is held in abeyance. The addict is called a patient rather
than an inmate, and he is given medication to ease his withdrawal from heroin. He also usually participates in group
discussions that are supposed to encourage groups of addicts
to face their problems and recognize narcotics use as a trap
rather than an escape.

But civil commitment really differs little from the routine imprisonment of convicts. The addict is locked up inside dismal, prison-like surroundings. He is put to work at an institutional trade. No new treatment experiments are carried out. The group discussions actually add little to the ineffectual revulsion that many addicts already feel about their habits. The result is that not long after their release many graduates of civil commitment return to heroin, crime, and, once again, the courts. When they land in court, they are liable for resumption of prosecution against them on the charge that first led to their civil commitment, as well as for any new crimes for which they have been arrested. The door remains unmistakably revolving.

Even the federal hospital at Lexington, the oldest of the civil-commitment facilities, has a dismal record of failure. The program in New York state, the largest in the country, has been criticized for its shabby facilities, the degrading and sometimes brutal treatment of patients, the abundance of problems typical of crowded prisons, such as homosexual attacks, and the inadequate training of young discussion-group leaders. Patients are led away from court to the treatment centers in handcuffs. Some treatment-center personnel have been arrested for mistreating patients. A New York City Criminal Court judge, Amos Basel, who once helped crusade for the state commitment program, concluded sadly after its first two years of existence that it "simply isn't supplying any answers" to the addiction problem. "I can't see any difference between this and a reformatory," Basel said.

Only two experimental systems have been credited with any small success in curbing addiction: voluntary abstinence groups engaging in their own brand of group therapy, which follow the model of Synanon in California, and the supplying of addicts with methadone, a man-made narcotic replacement for heroin. The self-help groups are somewhat similar to Alcoholics Anonymous, except that members usually find it necessary to live with the group—working, sleeping, and eating with other member-addicts—to continue successfully their abstinence. The vigilant group psychology serves as an alternative to the tight-knit, heroin-using fraternity of the street, whose members reinforce each other's dependence on drugs. But, because members of the abstinence groups find it difficult to leave them, this approach holds little hope for large-scale rehabilitation of hundreds of thousands of addicts.

Methadone, an inexpensive, synthetic narcotic administered legally in medically supervised experiments in several cities, can be used to treat addicts in large numbers. It is cheap, it can be taken orally in adequate dosages, and it does not create the debilitating physical and psychological problems that heroin does. However, it is also addictive. In effect, the patient becomes "hooked" on methadone itself. During treatment, urinalysis tests are necessary to be certain patients are not still taking heroin. Methadone relieves the addict's craving for heroin but does not create a physical revulsion to it, as researchers hope new drugs they are now experimenting with may do.

There is no doubt that much more research and experimentation is needed before effective ways of treating addiction are found. The search is made more difficult by the psychological dimension of addiction and its roots in the despair of city slums and the widespread uneasiness of our times. Use of heroin is even now spreading to elementary school children in the ghetto and among troubled high school youth in the affluent suburbs.

But the questions remain. Do we accomplish anything by continuing to drag addicts through the courts and prisons, where they find no help at all? Do we want to continue to underwrite the organized-crime monopoly of narcotics traffic and the resulting thievery committed by addicts to pay inflated black-market prices for drugs? A tip-off to what should be done is found in the way police in high-income areas handle the addicted children of the affluent. Rather than arresting these youths, the police notify their parents and help the children seek private hospitalization. But who will pay for this service for the poor? And where will the hospital space be found?

For years in Great Britain, it was legal for registered addicts to consume narcotics dispensed by prescription from physicians, while all other traffic in narcotics was prohibited. This kept narcotics largely out of the hands of criminals while making them available to addicts cheaply enough to afford without resorting to stealing. Abuses occurred, however, when doctors were persuaded to prescribe excessive amounts for registered addicts, who sold the excess to others. Britons became alarmed, too, about a recent rapid increase in the number of addicts in England from a few hundred about ten years ago to between 2,000 and 5,000 today. However, the response was not to prohibit possession of narcotics. Instead, in 1968, when private physicians were denied their authority to prescribe narcotics, free public drug-treatment centers were set up in their place—sixteen of them in London alone—where addicts now go for their narcotics supply and psychiatric counseling if they want it.

"Our immediate goal is not to cure the patient, but to find out all we can about addiction," a doctor at one clinic has said. There is still some illicit drug trafficking to supply those few addicts who do not want to be bothered by the formalities of the clinics. But there is no organized crime black market for narcotics in Great Britain because the clinic system satisfies most of the demand. As a result, despite a continuing increase in addicts and the recent appearance of a discernible addict subculture there, Great Britain has been spared the second and most threatening stage of the narcotics problem as experienced here: addict crime. Narcotics users in England commit no more crimes

than other citizens of similar social and economic back-
grounds.

A variation of the British system, attempted in the United
States between 1921 and 1925, is still referred to by advocates of tough narcotics laws as an example of the system's
impracticality. The clinics were closed after a scandal over
inefficiency in the huge New York City clinic. But "the
[specific] reasons for closing the clinics are obscure," a 1957
American Medical Association report concludes. Apparently,
officials panicked over the mainly administrative problems
of the New York clinic (which resulted in drugs being dispensed in overly large quantities) and disregarded the lack
of similar problems in other cities.

Many doctors now take a more liberal view of narcotics-
maintenance proposals and methadone-type maintenance
experiments than they did at that time, although some still
fear, as the law-enforcement establishment preaches, that
maintenance programs will sidetrack attempts to find "real
cures" for addiction. But this fear is unjustified if the medical profession is really willing to confront this critical pub-
lic-health problem with determination. Up to now, it has not
done so.

"The assertion that addicts are basically 'criminal types'
is unsound," Edwin Schur has noted. "If addicts are basically criminal, or if the drugs themselves cause criminal behavior, why do we find in Britain a low rate of addict crime?
All available evidence indicates that it is not addiction itself,
but the punitive approach to addiction, which produces
antisocial behavior in addicts."

Would it not be reasonable to stop labeling addicts as
criminals in the United States and to stop forcing them to
prey on others to cope with their dependency on drugs?
That addiction would be dramatically curtailed by making
supervised dispensing of cheap narcotics legal is quite unlikely. But it is equally unlikely that any other steps will

decrease addiction until medical research provides more answers. In the meantime, scrapping our punitive, unworkable approach to the problem—and possibly adopting some type of mixed system of drug- and methadone-dispensing centers—could sharply reduce addict crime, as well as provide humane treatment for addicts themselves. So long as the problem continues to be dumped in the criminal courts, the results will continue to be increased frustrations in the already overburdened courts, more suffering for society, and more profit and power for the nation's organized crime juggernaut.

The rapid growth and robust economic health of organized crime in the United States is one of the most odious by-products of revolving-door criminal laws. Although it is now diversified, organized crime still thrives on the economic monopolies it enjoys because of the illegality of narcotics usage, gambling, prostitution, and the like. The impetus given organized crime in the United States during Prohibition through trafficking in illegal alcoholic beverages should not be forgotten. Although sale and possession of liquor was illegal, the public demand for it never waned. Formerly law-abiding citizens committed criminal acts freely and frequently, and lifelong criminals made fortunes in bootlegging. Today, narcotics have replaced bootleg liquor, and the heroin subculture of the street serves as a latter-day equivalent of the speak-easy.

But even more important financially to organized crime than the narcotics traffic is illegal gambling, with an annual volume estimated to be as high as $50 billion. The widespread public acceptance of gambling, coupled with its prohibition in most forms in most states, provides organized crime with its most lucrative enterprise and the criminal courts with another burden of ridiculous proportions. Although more than 100,000 persons are arrested for gambling each year, the law enforcement effort has failed completely to discourage illegal betting.

Instead, the courts are inundated with an unmanageable volume of cases in which justice can seldom be done. Almost everyone bets at one time or another with friends on an athletic contest or in a poker game. But the effects of enforcement are once again felt mostly by slum dwellers, who patronize betting shops that are highly conspicuous to the police.

Several cities, including New York and Chicago, maintain separate, crowded gambling courts, in which, as in drunk and narcotics courts, the mass processing of defendants is even more hasty and cynical than in other criminal-court branches. Conviction and punishment almost never deters the offender. Judges, who are often known to make a bet themselves now and then, seldom give stiff sentences to gamblers. The question they sometimes ask themselves is, Is justice done when a man who places or takes bets, doing no harm to anyone else, is sent to jail?

The only possible inherent danger in gambling is the threat of great losses to persons who overextend their finances or are cheated by the operator of the game. If gambling were legalized and had state supervision, these potential problems could be minimized.

Legalizing gambling could channel into the public coffers money that now goes to criminals. Federal or state governments could run off-track-betting operations, lotteries, and the like, or they could license private firms to do it. Legalized bingo operates smoothly this way now in many states. New York and Massachusetts already have begun state lotteries. In 1970, New York City began conducting off-track betting through a public benefit corporation. Nevada has long licensed and taxed privately operated gambling of many kinds. The reach of organized crime could be limited somewhat by competition from legalized private or public gambling operations.

Prostitution, another mainstay of organized crime syndicates, presents a court problem similar to gambling. Despite centuries of on-again, off-again legal harassment, prostitution has always flourished. Today, arrest, followed by a court fine or short stay in jail, is regarded by violators as an expected inconvenience of their work. And organized crime, which offers prostitutes protection from the police, once again is enriched.

The one undeniable public danger of prostitution, the spread of venereal disease, is unchecked by present law enforcement. If prostitution were legalized, prostitutes would be less frightened about turning to health authorities for treatment of disease. In fact, in European countries, prostitutes licensed by the government transmit venereal diseases less frequently than the rest of the population.

Moral and legal problems are often created by the methods used by police to enforce criminal laws against gambling and prostitution. Unless there are complaining victims, the police have a difficult time making a case against violators. So they resort to bursting into homes on raids, tapping telephone lines, and entrapping offenders by posing as customers. These are the kinds of police practices that can most often lead to abuses and unnecessary invasion of the privacy of innocent persons. In Washington, D.C., policewomen (dubbed "flat-foot floozies") were recently used as bait to entrap men looking for prostitutes. One suburbanite successfully fought his arrest in court, but only after the incident had cost him his top-secrecy security clearance, his government job, and his wife. What is more, these borderline enforcement methods usually produce nothing more than a brief inconvenience for the professional gambler or prostitute.

Today's most repugnant law enforcement practices, however, are those visited on homosexuals, whose natural sexual inclinations, even if fulfilled entirely in private with another consenting adult, still constitute a crime in American society and lead to the most dismaying revolving-door cases for our courts. Entrapment is usually the only way a homosexual can be "caught" breaking the law. Policemen dressed in tight-fitting, flashy clothes pose as homosexuals in bars, parks, and public washrooms and arrest anyone who appears to respond to their advances. If this technique fails, police often round up suspected homosexuals on vague "vagrancy" charges. Often blackmailers, posing as police officers, use the illegality of homosexuality as a license for their own kind of crime.

It should not be necessary to point out that no sufficient legal or moral case can be made in the first place for legal prohibition of private homosexual acts between consenting adult partners or that experience as a criminal defendant cannot seriously be expected to "reform" a homosexual. Why, moreover, should it?

The same question can be asked about the less frequent arrests of adults who engage in private heterosexual extramarital relations, group sex activities, or "unnatural" sex acts. Laws prohibiting these activities are broken daily. Enforcement occurs only rarely, but the absurd threat of it is always there.

Some overriding questions must be asked about all these cases of misapplication of the criminal sanction: Who is going to respect laws that prohibit conduct condoned by large numbers of citizens and which of itself visits harm on no one? What effect does widespread disrespect and occasional harsh enforcement of these laws have on the nation's life? Why further swamp our already crowded courts with pointless prosecution of these cases?

The Law Enforcement Task Force of the National Commission on the Causes and Prevention of Violence recently suggested the following reason for the surprising lawlessness of many Americans:

The criminal sanction is society's most drastic tool for regulating conduct. When it is used against conduct that a large segment of society considers normal, and which is not seriously harmful to others, contempt for the law is encouraged. When it is used against conduct that is involuntary and the result of illness, the law becomes inhumane.

It concluded that

. . . only when the load of law enforcement has been lightened by stripping away those responsibilities for which it is not suited will we begin to make the criminal law a more effective instrument of social protection.

Giving the criminal courts responsibilities for shaping social behavior that they can never succeed in carrying out only increases the inability of the courts to administer true justice—and stop the revolving doors.

IV

"We Poor Against a Powerful Rich"

Charles Baker, a black man in his forties, has worked half his life for the Campbell Soup Company in Chicago. He is still a relatively low-paid factory worker; by any realistic standards, he and his family are poor.

Nevertheless, Baker was able to save a little money, and, a few years ago, he welcomed the opportunity offered by a realtor selling small row houses on Chicago's West Side. Baker was told he needed only to make a down payment of a few hundred dollars and sign a contract for additional monthly payments to the realtor. He could rent out half of the house to help make these payments. After several years, the realtor promised, Baker would qualify to get a mortgage loan and could begin buying title to the home.

Only later did Baker find out that he had been tricked, along with hundreds of his black neighbors in the crowded West Side section of Lawndale. Dishonest real estate operators had doubled the prices of the small houses on the contracts the families signed and then charged exorbitant interest on top of that. Most Lawndale families wound up owing four times the real value of their homes, and eventually they were told they had little chance of ever qualifying for the mortgage loans necessary actually to purchase title.

The experience was not altogether new for the families of

Lawndale. They had been cheated before in the ghetto—by slum landlords in the rundown tenements from which they had come, credit clothing and appliance merchants who gouged them on installment payments for inferior goods, insurance companies that charged everyone in that part of the city higher rates, and countless others. The low-income blacks had come to expect such treatment and had learned to live with it.

But this time they were offered unexpected hope of redress. Young Jesuit novices working at a Lawndale parish persuaded Baker and his neighbors to fight back in court, where all Americans are promised justice. Together, they formed the Contract Buyers League and sued the realtors and their financial backers for fraud and racial discrimination. For months, the court suit dragged on while Lawndale residents continued to make their monthly payments.

Finally, Baker and other Contract Buyers League leaders decided to refuse to pay any more, in an attempt to force the realtors to renegotiate their contracts immediately. But, as soon as the payments stopped, the realtors simply went to court to evict for nonpayment the scores of families who were withholding their monthly installments. Baker and his neighbors then returned to court to ask the judge to prevent their eviction on the grounds that the realtors had no right to charge them so much in the first place and that they had sold the houses under false pretenses. The Lawndale residents wanted the judge to sanction their holdout so that the realtors would be forced to bargain. Their day in court, however, turned out to be shattering.

"I had the privilege to see how the courts operate, and it's terrible," Baker said after his experience inside the towering new glass and steel courthouse in Chicago. "If you're behind on your note and want to explain, forget it. They only want your name, address, and to ask, 'Are you behind on your payments?' "

Baker and others asked for an opportunity to explain to a jury why they thought the realtors were acting illegally. But the judge ruled in every case that the law was clearly on the realtors' side and that nothing was left for a jury to decide. The Lawndale families must pay up or lose their homes, he ordered.

"The judge operated by the law," Baker said later. "And the law evicts poor people from their homes."

The law also forces the poor man to pay the ghetto merchant every penny of excessive installment-payment interest but gives the buyer no recourse if he discovers he was overcharged or if the merchandise is faulty, the workmanship shoddy, or the job left unfinished. Under the law in most states, slum tenants can do little or nothing if their landlords fail to keep their housing safe, sanitary, or heated in the winter, but the law protects the landlord's right to collect rent every month, raise the rent whenever he wants to, and evict tenants at any time, for any reason. The law pushes poor people out of their homes to facilitate urban renewal, makes them endure countless indignities to collect welfare benefits, and leaves them with public schooling and health-care services that are nearly always inferior to those provided in higher-income neighborhoods.

The courts usually enforce these property laws strictly. They also charge a prohibitively high price of admission in filing and legal fees for poor people who wish to exercise their legal right to fight back. And they thwart those who do get inside the courthouse—by procedures and traditions that favor the rich, the businessman, and the government.

"What chance have we poor against a powerful rich?" a black man in New York asked law professor Jerome E. Carlin. To that man and most of the other poor people interviewed by Carlin for his recent monograph on lower-class attitudes about American justice, the law and the courts are at best irrelevant—institutions that do not apply to the poor or that deal with them arbitrarily as virtual nonpersons when they are singled out as crime victims, accused criminals, or tenants whom a landlord is trying to evict. Worse, the poor consider the law and the courts to be powerful tools frequently used by those who exploit, oppress, and humiliate them.

Yet, as the National Commission on the Causes and Prevention of Violence has pointed out, "the last resort of the poor as well as the rich is in the courts." The Commission warned that the courts "must stand between the individual citizen and the carnivorous merchant, the profiteering landlord, the arbitrary administrator. If he cannot find justice there, the poor man is lost."

The courts now leave the poor so bewildered, Carlin has found in his surveys, that the more often a poor man has been inside a courtroom the less likely he is to return voluntarily to press a legitimate claim he may have arising from an accident or a financial transaction. "The poor man's experience with the law is hardly rewarding," according to Carlin. "Instead of reinforcing a commitment to use the law to assert and protect his rights, his legal encounters may increase his alienation from the legal system." In other words, he simply gets tired of losing.

"To the poor man," the late Senator Robert F. Kennedy, a former U.S. Attorney General, once observed, " 'legal' has become a synonym for technicalities and obstructions, not for that which is to be respected. The poor man looks upon the law as an enemy, not as a friend. For him, the law is always taking something away."

Overwhelming frustration and hopelessness, and a feeling that the law is meant for somebody else, can help lead to anarchy and violence, as in the rioting and burning in Charles Baker's West Side Chicago neighborhood and others like it across the nation. During the troubled summers of the past decade, the rioters' primary targets have been the ghetto merchants, who had always stood impregnably behind the law in their dishonest business dealings, and the police, who serve as the most visible symbol of the law in the inner city.

"The twin problems of racism and poverty have converged in our society to become the problem of the inner city itself," Judge J. Skelly Wright, of the U.S. Court of Appeals for the District of Columbia, wrote in the *New York Times Magazine* (March 9, 1969).

Lack of equal opportunity has given black Americans a disproportionately large share of poverty, and the legal discrimination that persists for poor people serves to prolong for the poor among black citizens the racial discrimination of the past. Such discrimination is no longer lawful, but the law serves to support it. However, the frustration of poor blacks barely exceeds that of the Spanish-American poor in northern ghettos and southern migrant worker camps, the whites in lingering pockets of poverty elsewhere, or the nation's great mass of lower-income blue-collar workers. They, too, find that the law and courts seem to penalize them for being poor and to frustrate their attempts to better themselves or to fight injustice.

To begin with, the very substance of our laws works inevitably against equal justice for the poor. As Carlin points out, the law has historically "been oriented toward the protection of property" and those who hold property and economic power. Thus, it "benefits and protects sellers over buyers, lenders over borrowers, and landlords over tenants." A tenant's obligation to pay rent has always been independent of any contractual obligation of a landlord to provide habitable housing. A creditor need only prove the existence of a debt, not its legitimacy, to collect it. A seller does not have to prove that his product or service is what the buyer expected—or even that it has any worth at all—to exercise his right to payment. In each case, the burden rests with the tenant, the debtor, or the buyer to prove that he has been wronged. Even then, the law often allows him no recourse and blames him for making a bad bargain. The poor, of course, are always the tenant, the debtor, the buyer. They do not write the laws, nor are they powerful constituents of those who do. The poor are legally disadvantaged.

Businessmen receiving government subsidies are treated as legal equals of the government, but poor people are stripped of many of their legal rights when they become welfare recipients. Usury laws are very flexible for many kinds of lenders, especially those lending to the poor; they can find all sorts of loopholes that enable them to charge higher rates of interest than the apparent statutory limit. But debtors are invariably required to pay what the lender demands.

One especially onerous legal device that gives the seller a big legal advantage over the buyer, and makes possible wholesale exploitation of the poor, is something known as the "holder in due course." When an individual buys a product or service on installment payments and the installment note is sold by the merchant to a third-party finance company or bank for collection, that third party becomes the holder in due course. Its right to collect on the note is protected by law from any claim by the customer that he was cheated in the original transaction. Thus, when a poor man buys an appliance, piece of furniture, car, home improvement, or other product or service, he more often than not must agree to sign to pay for it in installments. But later, if he discovers that the product is faulty, the service was not performed as promised, or the price is grossly in excess of value, and would like to stop payment to force the seller to rectify matters, he usually finds that he no longer owes the money to the merchant. Rather, he is in debt to a finance company or bank that bought the installment payment note from the merchant. The high price that the contract charges the customer is usually what the finance company pays the merchant for the note, assuring the merchant a large profit. The finance company's profit is the interest on the contract, which is included in the installment payments it collects from the customer. As the third party, or holder in due course, the finance company has a legal right to full payment from the customer, no matter how badly he may have been cheated. If the customer does not pay, the creditor may repossess the product, if any; sue for default; appropriate (garnish) the buyer's wages; take any security that was pledged; or ruin the buyer's credit rating.

The only way the customer can try to get what he thought he was paying for is to go to court himself and sue the merchant. He then often learns that the merchant operated through a fly-by-night front firm, which has changed its name and location or left town. Even if the merchant can be brought into court, it is difficult, time-consuming, and costly for the customer to prove fraud—much more difficult than it is, for instance, for the holder in due course to prove in court that the customer is indebted to him. As a result, the poor man must pay what is demanded, which is often too much, for a defective TV set, an inferior sofa, a misrepresented automobile, or a shoddy roofing job.

The abuses of the holder-in-due-course doctrine are well known to the legal community. One judge has called it "the mask behind which fraud hides." Many unscrupulous businessmen simply set up dummy finance companies to which they appear to sell their installment-payment contracts. These front finance companies claim legal immunity to complaints from cheated customers. The chicanery here, too, is hard to prove, and seldom do the courts bother to try. Seldom, either, do poor litigants have the resources to force the issue.

Nine states have modified their holder-in-due-course laws, but the "reform" consists simply of requiring notification to the buyer that the finance company has bought the contract and that the buyer has a few days in which to state and have acted on any complaints he may have. This notification can be difficult for the buyer to understand, if it ever reaches him, and it gives him little if any recourse unless he has become aware of fraud before or during the brief ten- or fifteen-day warning period granted him.

With the disgraceful exception of the holder-in-due-course doctrine, it would appear that contract law treats alike the poor and rich, buyer and seller, debtor and creditor. After all, both signers of a contract are equally obligated in theory by the agreement therein. But it does not always work that way in practice. Very seldom do the poor understand the language of contracts as well as those writing and tendering them. Often, the crowded pieces of paper contain complicated clauses giving the seller outlandish rights or taking other rights away from the buyer. One of these, frequently used by ghetto merchants, is known as a "confession of judgment." By signing, the buyer agrees that if he misses one payment, the seller can repossess the merchandise immediately—without notice, court hearing, or a judge's order. Another much more insidious clause allows the seller to repossess not only the particular item covered in the contract at hand, but also anything else the buyer has purchased from the seller and is still making installment payments on. In the ghetto, many families buy one item after another from a particular merchant only because he is the one who will extend credit to them. In many cases, the merchant encourages the customer to overextend himself and continues to give further credit, in certain knowledge that in the end he will reap a bonanza.

A celebrated Washington, D.C., case shows how this scheme works and how the law allows it to flourish. Over a five-year period, a furniture store in the Washington slums sold $1,800 worth of furniture and appliances to a mother on relief, Mrs. Ora Lee Williams. Salesmen at the store showed her how she could pay for it all in a series of small, if seemingly endless, installment payments. On top of this, the store sold her a stereo set on still another installment contract, with the full realization, as the store's credit records later showed, that this purchase was what would finally put Mrs. Williams in over her head. The contract Mrs. Williams signed for the stereo included, as had the others before it, that pernicious clause, which, in effect, gave the store the right to repossess everything she had not yet finished paying for. At the time of the stereo purchase, Mrs. Williams owed only $170 of the original $1,800. Yet, when she missed a single payment on the stereo, the store took back every bit of the furniture. Thus it ended up with nearly $1,800 from Mrs. Williams, five years of installment interest, *and* all the furniture it had sold her.

In the ghetto, stories like Mrs. Williams's are common. But for once, in her case, help was offered and a rare victory was won. Lawyers of the Washington, D.C., Neighborhood Legal Services project, one of many groups in the nation funded by the Office of Economic Opportunity (OEO) to provide free legal aid for the poor, sued the store. The local courts said that nothing could be done to stop the practice: The law clearly enforces whatever is contained in a signed contract. But the U.S. Court of Appeals for the District of Columbia caused a stir in Washington's legal community by reversing the lower court decisions and giving Mrs. Williams back her furniture. U.S. Court of Appeals Judge J. Skelly Wright noted in the *Times* that the operative clause in Mrs. Williams's contract with the furniture store was an "obscure, almost unintelligible fine-print provision" that was difficult even for lawyers to understand. He noted that this was one of the few times that any U.S. court, contrary to all legal precedent, had allowed a low-income buyer to default on a contract because the contract was unfairly drawn in the first place.

Those who exploit the poor default on their contractual obligations with impunity all the time. Ghetto merchants refuse to honor written warranties. Landlords fail to keep housing up to code standards. Insurance companies cancel policies before their terms have expired to avoid paying claims. In some cases, these parties to a contract are acting legally through loopholes in the law; in others, they are flaunting the law without effective challenge.

"It is no coincidence that law schools teach courses in creditors' rights, not debtors' rights; in property rights, not welfare rights," Jerome Carlin notes. "Even if law schools wanted to stress the law of the poor instead of the law of the rich, they would find themselves short of law to teach because, generally speaking, it has not been developed to meet the needs of the poor."

In carrying out the law, the courts also continue to treat the poor as inherently inferior to other litigants. Those courtrooms that the poor perforce frequent—for small-claims suits and landlord and tenant disputes, for instance—are terribly crowded, located in the poorest facilities, and are the most understaffed of all civil courts. The litigants are treated patronizingly by court officials and their cases rushed through. Judges maintain less decorum and observe fewer rules of procedure in these courts, except when the enforcement of certain rules helps to move a case more quickly. The poor are not expected to have lawyers, and seldom is anything resembling a full-scale trial ever held. The poor man's civil court and the quality of what passes for justice inside it differs little from the crowded criminal courtrooms not far away, where the poor man is also given short shrift.

Small-claims court was originally created for the poor man. Here he was to be able to confront others in legal disputes involving a few hundred dollars or less to collect money owed him or to sue merchants who had cheated him. Nominal filing fees were set as low as a dollar or two in most cities. Lawyers were not required, and rules of evidence and procedure were kept informal to enable the poor man to speak for himself more easily. But it was not long before businessmen discovered that small-claims court could work instead to their advantage. There, with relatively little expense, they could sue to collect small unpaid and disputed debts from the poor. They sent in legions of lawyers to handle their cases, forced judges to invoke legal rules when it was to the businessman's advantage, and, in general, made the contest with the unrepresented poor unequal again. A court created for the poor man, to avoid those inequities he suffered in other parts of the legal system, began to be operated, like the rest, for the convenience of his adversaries.

Today, in most big cities, the poor seldom bother to file cases in small-claims courts. Instead, studies show, 80 to 90 per cent of the cases are filed by business firms: merchants, collection agencies, finance companies, and utilities. They file and win their cases in the same wholesale numbers, using small-claims courts as government-financed collection agencies.

The small-claims court equivalent of a trial usually consists of the lawyer for the plaintiff showing the judge proof of the debt—an installment contract, unpaid bill, or the like. The defendant, usually not represented by a lawyer, has only one defense: proof that he has already paid the debt. If he admits not paying, the judge usually does not allow him to argue that he has been cheated or that the debt is larger than he was led to believe it would be. The result most often is that the creditor's lawyer persuades the defendant to accept a "compromise" that reduces the debt by a small fraction and gives the debtor new terms under which to pay it off.

Only when the defendant is represented by a lawyer does the outcome differ. Studies show that, when defendants come to court with attorneys, claims against them in the majority of cases are cut in half or dismissed outright. Collection lawyers for creditors, however, try to postpone the case if the defendant has a lawyer or when, as sometimes happens, the judge on the small-claims bench that day is one who occasionally tries to bend the law to enlarge the debtor's rights. The next time the case comes up, the collection lawyer may have things more his way. If he wins the case in the end, he also is entitled to collect from the defendant the court and legal costs accruing from the delay he himself staged.

Cases that require any courtroom work at all for the collection lawyer are, however, the exception. In nine out of every ten small-claims cases, the defendant never shows up and the creditor wins his judgment by default. For hours, the court clerk simply calls one case after another. "Ready, your honor," the collection lawyer announces. No defendant comes forward. "Judgment for the plaintiff," the judge orders in a monotone. "Judgment for the plaintiff . . . judgment for the plaintiff" is repeated again and again and again in the sleepy courtroom.

Undoubtedly, many defendants do not show up because they are continuing to evade payment of a debt they know they owe. Some others must believe it makes no difference whether they go or not. But the majority fail to show up in court simply because they did not know they were supposed to. In many cases, they were never even notified that they were sued.

In some jurisdictions, notice of the suit must only be

mailed, and it often reaches the wrong address. In many more others, marshals or private process-servers hired by creditors are supposed to hand the summonses to the defendants personally. But often they throw them away instead. Among lawyers, this is called "sewer service." A New York City study showed recently that at least two of every three summonses for debt cases never reach the defendants for this reason.

Once the creditor has won his judgment in small-claims court, he is entitled to collect his award any way he can. The most popular and effective method is garnishment of the defendant's wages at work. The debtor's employer is directed by the court to take a certain amount out of each paycheck and turn it over to the creditor. This practice, of course, takes away what little remains of the poor man's bargaining power in a case where he believes the court judgment against him was unjust, should he want to fight it by continued withholding payment. Often, the order of garnishment costs the debtor his job. Many employers of low-paid, easily replaced workers do not want to go to the trouble or expense of transferring and accounting for the money.

In New York City, Carlin reports finding, garnishment is often carried out illegally by the city marshal's office. The marshal is directed by law to investigate whether selling some of the defendant's property will satisfy the judgment without garnishment. "The marshal's income," Carlin reports, "is totally derived from fees, however, and he appears eager to dispose of his cases rapidly. Consequently he sometimes moves directly to garnishment without investigation of the defendant's property at all."

In some states, creditors were able for many years to begin garnishment upon filing of the court complaint, long before judgment was won. This became illegal when the

U.S. Supreme Court ruled in 1969 that some court hearing must be held before a judge could order garnishment. The right to a hearing is an empty one, however, if the defendant is not properly notified so that he can be there, too, to try to protect himself.

The successful plaintiff in small-claims court is often a ghetto merchant suing to enforce a questionable installment contract against an overextended buyer. A Federal Trade Commission (FTC) study in Washington, D.C., showed that in 1966 just eleven ghetto merchants collected 2,690 small-claims-court judgments against their customers—one judgment for every $2,200 of sales. These merchants, the FTC found, charged 60 per cent more for comparable or even inferior goods than did sellers outside the ghetto and used high-interest installment-payment contracts three times more often. The ghetto merchants claim they must charge more to cover losses from customers who do not pay.

But the FTC study showed that these merchants, and the finance companies and collection agencies behind them, seldom lose. Instead, they count on small-claims court to help them draw a vicious circle in which they trap their ghetto customers: entice them with merchandise and seemingly low installment payments, obtain their signatures on installment contracts with exorbitant charges and catch-all repossession rights, saddle them with more payments than they can keep up with, collect what money they can pay, and then sue them after the first missed payment for repossession and whatever more money that can be collected.

When the system is really humming, the customer suddenly finds his furniture or car gone, considerably less money in his pay envelope, or himself out of job—often without ever knowing in advance that he had been sued. "It's a miracle they don't burn down the courthouse," said a judge who takes turns on the small-claims bench in Washington, D.C., where most of the defendants are poor blacks. "All they see is white people enforcing white laws designed to do them in."

Although it seems almost impossible, conditions are frequently even worse for the poor man in landlord and tenant court, which was also designed originally to help the poor by assuring the existence of a forum for evenhanded legal bargaining between monied landlords and poor tenants. Now it, too, is little more than a collection agency, in which hundreds of tenants—most of whom do not appear in court —are ordered evicted from their homes by a judge each day in every U.S. city.

The volume of cases in landlord and tenant court in most cities is staggering, running into the hundreds daily. Most are filed by landlords to force tenants to pay rent or to evict them. The landlord's lawyer must only tell the judge that the landlord wants to evict and has given the required notice or that the tenant is behind in his rent. As in small-claims court, most defendants do not show up and default judgment is ordered. If the tenant does come to court, he finds that there is nothing much he can say to the judge to affect the outcome of the case. If he owes rent, he must pay, no matter what. If the landlord wants to evict him for some reason, that is the landlord's legal right. Any complaints that the tenant may have about his living conditions are immaterial here. Complaints must be reported to the city inspectors and the process for redress with this department—in most cities, an inefficient bureaucracy—is slow and frustrating. One wonders why landlord and tenant court meets at all. Nothing is contested. Why doesn't somebody sitting in an office simply write out a court order to evict whenever a landlord requests it?

When tenants take complaints about housing conditions to city officials, they are told that inspectors will check on

them and order landlords to comply with the housing code.
But, unlike tenants, landlords find they can outwait or evade
the law. A tenant who dawdles in carrying out his end of
the contract—paying rent—is usually quickly evicted by the
courts. A landlord usually is allowed a long grace period to
comply "voluntarily" after a housing inspector orders repairs or is granted extensions on the repair order by the
city. A study in New York City showed that landlords there
stall for an average of five months before the city steps in.
In Chicago, 85 per cent of the housing repair orders are
extended at least once, and the majority at least three
times. In most cities, the government finally files criminal
charges against the landlord for noncompliance. But the
prosecutor then gives the landlord still more time to act to
have the charges dropped. In Washington, D.C., many cases
have languished two years from the time the housing inspector first noted a violation of the housing code until the
landlord was finally brought before a judge to answer
charges of noncompliance.

Landlords seldom are sent to jail after being found guilty
of disobeying city orders to repair their buildings. The sentence is usually a nominal fine. Even then, the landlord may
pay the fine and still not make repairs. Instead of protecting
the poor man's meager legal rights, the law and the courts
once again are instrumental in keeping him chained to a
treadmill. The poor have little choice as to where they can
live; they are left with what no one else wants. They cannot wait until an apartment is put in perfect condition before they move in. They cannot insist on a lease that protects
their interests. When a tenant does sign a lease, he often
agrees unwittingly to clauses that authorize imposition of
high penalty charges for late rent payments, exculpate the
landlord of liability for injuries the tenant may suffer as a
result of disrepair, make the tenant responsible for many
repairs, or impose unreasonable prohibitions against dis-

turbances by tenants and even restrictions on visitors they may receive. The tenant is virtually powerless to do anything to force his landlord to fulfill his legal responsibility to keep the housing up to code standards.

The frequent result is that old or badly repaired plaster falls from ceilings and walls. Unvarnished floors rot away. Water pipes leak and rupture, and the dampness caves in boards underfoot or overhead. Jumbled electrical wiring blows fuses that are not replaced. Furnaces fail to work. Water often stops running or comes out of the hot tap cold. Repairs that are made still leave eyesores—bulges of replaced plaster, bowed walls and ceilings, cheap, drab or garishly colored paint that flakes and peels almost immediately.

Meanwhile, the law and the courts, presumed sources and protectors of justice, stand behind the landlord in almost anything he does and provide poor tenants with little recourse. Ironically, the situation worsens when, under public pressure, the courts enforce housing code compliance more vigorously without otherwise improving the tenant's bargaining position. A landlord faced with the inevitability of making expensive repairs to continue renting out his housing simply evicts his tenants and boards up his property. While his tenants are homeless, he can then wait for the opportunity to make other use of his holdings. Thousands of slum buildings have been left this way in the nation's big cities, further limiting the poor man's supply of housing. The courts can only penalize the landlord for not repairing those buildings that he is renting; they cannot force him to keep buildings on the market.

Some states have sought to give tenants the right to withhold rent if the landlord does not maintain housing. In New York, tenants can pay the rent to the court instead. But this still does not ensure that the landlord will make repairs, and the tenant must still pay out his rent money to someone without the satisfaction of receiving decent housing in return. A few other states allow tenants to contract for repairs themselves and withhold the cost from their rent. But most of these laws restrict the amount the tenant can use this way to one month's rent, which is seldom enough to make most neglected slum apartments fit for habitation. Moreover, in every case, the landlord is still free to evict troublemaking tenants. The law gives him that right, and the courts enforce it.

The law also frequently pushes poor people out of their houses when the government, federal or local, decides to "renew" neighborhoods of dilapidated housing. The slum landlord is paid by the government for his rotting or long-ago abandoned building. But the tenants are usually moved out without reparation, and they are unlikely to find new homes in the neighborhood. Luxury apartments, offices, and highways generally appear on the site of their old homes. Tens of thousands of poor people have been displaced this way in American cities during the past two decades.

The first urban renewal laws were passed just after World War II. Since then, amendments to these laws have required the government to relocate displaced families in decent housing. But, unlike poor people, the government can get away with violating the law. Displaced poor families often are confronted with long waiting lists, moves that would take them across the city from their old neighborhoods and jobs, relocation housing that is in substandard condition, or even no new home at all.

Because there was nowhere else for them to go, families living in the deteriorated Northgate section of Camden, New Jersey, during the late 1960's, remained in their old homes even as demolition for urban renewal was under way all around them. They were inundated by fleeing rats and threatened by flash fires and collapsing buildings. The

Camden urban renewal authority had lied to the federal government about how much relocation housing was available when the government gave the city permission to start the federally supported renewal program. Newark, New Jersey, claimed in 1967 to have more than 3,500 vacancies available for families forced out of its urban renewal areas. One third turned out to be housing in other neighborhoods scheduled for urban renewal clearance or new highways in the near future. Another 10 per cent were found to be unfit for human habitation.

State courts claim they can do little to force governments to obey the federal urban renewal law. The federal courts, meanwhile, have not yet recognized an individual citizen's right to sue to enforce the relocation requirements of the law.

The courts also allow the government, when it is acting as landlord itself, to behave as arbitrarily and callously as cynical slumlords. In the crowded public housing projects of big cities, conditions sometimes resemble those in the most run-down privately owned slum buildings. But the government does not serve housing violation notices on itself. Public housing authorities have even more legal leeway to evict tenants without reason than have private landlords. They raise rents whenever they choose. Tenants must put up with conditions or leave. The courts allow tenants no rights and uphold everything the government does. In landlord and tenant courts in many cities, the largest volume of cases for collection of back rent and eviction of tenants are filed and won by the government itself.

Just as creditors have captured small-claims court and landlords have come to dominate landlord and tenant court, government bureaucrats now run public housing to serve their needs rather than those of the poor. Officials must keep costs down and minimize problem situations. Long waiting lists make it a seller's market. Public housing was created as an emergency means of providing the very poor with the decent housing guaranteed all Americans by the Housing Act of 1949. But the bureaucrats have let maintenance slide, raised rents to nearly the level of rents in the ghettos, and dealt with and evicted tenants arbitrarily. The law and the courts help make such scandalous and callous conduct possible.

Almost as though it were a law of nature, every program devised for the benefit of the poor seems destined to be captured by another interest and twisted, with no interference from the courts, until it works against the poor. This tragic principle is perhaps best illustrated by the workings of the national welfare system.

To begin with, welfare recipients are not the only citizens who receive government aid, and they receive less than most. Invaluable airwave rights are granted to owners of radio and television stations. Docks and airports are built for shippers and airline owners. Cash is paid to farmers and many transportation firms. Money is loaned at subsidized rates and with government insurance to small-businessmen, builders, and home buyers. Various tax deductions worth billions in the aggregate are granted to many kinds of monied citizens and businesses. Laws passed by Congress have given these citizens a right to government handouts. The courts protect their rights. Nobody required any of these citizens or businesses to give up anything in return for what is given them. The agencies of the U.S. Government that dole out these subsidies are usually responsible and responsive to the interests of their clients—as is, for instance, the Federal Housing Administration to builders—and the courts ensure that accountability.

Yet, as Judge Wright of the U.S. Court of Appeals for the District of Columbia has written, "despite the pervasiveness of public assistance throughout our economy, only the welfare recipient is singled out for special, degrading supervision and control." Wealthy farmers, Wright points out, qualify for crop-support payments on the theory that an imbalance in our economy would otherwise cause them unwarranted financial harm. They do not have to become paupers to receive government checks.

The urban poor, even more than the farmer, are victims of a national economic imbalance. Welfare was envisioned as a way for easing some of the suffering that resulted. But in the view of many better-off Americans, the welfare recipient is somebody who is getting something for nothing—a beggar, not a citizen with the same rights as others. The policies of our welfare agencies reflect this view. Their client class is not really the poor, whom they ostensibly serve, but rather the middle-class bureaucrats who staff the agencies and the middle-class citizens who pay their salaries. Welfare rules and procedures are made for them—to satisfy their sensibilities and keep their costs down—rather than for the poor.

Before becoming eligible for welfare, a poor man or woman must be out of work, depleted of savings, without an automobile or the common household appliances taken for granted by middle-class Americans, and unable to be supported by relatives. He or she must prove all of this to the government, and even then eligibility may be denied. The eligibility system, after all, is designed to help keep the middle-class citizen assured that the fewest possible persons are receiving welfare, not to assure that the most people who need help will get it.

"We have set up every conceivable kind of barrier to exclude or discourage the desperately poor from even [minimal] level of aid," one welfare expert, Elizabeth Wickenden, said at a 1965 national conference on law and poverty convened by the federal government. She cited arbitrary limits on age, length of local residence, employability, existence of a relative who could support the applicant, and the like.

For every one name added to welfare rolls, one or more is denied. Of the 8.5 million people on welfare in the United States, less than 80,000 are employable adult men. The majority of the recipients are children.

Staying on the welfare rolls can be an agonizing experience. Investigators are deployed to spot cheating, and recipients must be prepared at any time to allow searches of their homes. Until recently, mothers receiving welfare aid for their children were not allowed to have men living in their houses, and investigators were free to drop by in the middle of the night to make certain the rule was being obeyed. Benefits can be withdrawn for reasons that the recipient is never given a chance to dispute. Overpayments due to the agency's error can be collected back at any time. The welfare department has a lien on any small amount a recipient may leave to an heir. By obtaining a job, even if the income leaves him well below real subsistence level, the recipient works his way out of government assistance. Periodically, budget-balancing state governments, which dole out federal money matched by funds of their own, cut back on welfare payments across the board, as New York and California have done recently. Southern states keep eligibility tight and payments low, forcing many poor families to move north.

"Welfare policies tend to cast the recipient in the role of the propertyless, shiftless pauper," concluded the report of the Moreland Commission on the administration of public welfare in New York. Any property, any stake in life he may have had must be exhausted or turned over to the welfare department before he is eligible for assistance. The report pointed out:

> This implies he is incompetent and inadequate to meet the demands of competitive life. He is then regarded as if he had little or no feelings, aspirations, or normal sensibilities. This process of proving and maintaining eligibility in combination

with the literal adherence to regulations and procedures tends to produce a self-perpetuating system of dependency and dehumanization.

Between the welfare department and the public housing authority, the welfare recipient is told by the government where to live, with whom to live, how much and what kind of food to buy, what other "necessities" to buy if money is left over, and, even (in the case of one welfare mother whose eight-year-old son was struck and killed by a truck), which funeral home to call—the one with which the welfare department has a contract. Welfare, according to a Presidential commission, is "life-long probation."

In most states, poor persons are added to and taken off welfare roles or forced to do certain things to remain on welfare, without any right to a hearing or any other means of protesting harmful or unwarranted government action. The courts have refused to extend to welfare recipients the same legal rights enjoyed by others who receive government assistance.

"It is a double standard from the moral point of view and a double standard from the legal point of view," concluded Yale law professor Charles Reich in a January, 1965, *Yale Law Journal* article. "There is a law for the poor and a law for the rest of us. Receipt of government aid by the poor carries a stigma, whereas receipt of government aid by the rest of the economy has been made into a virtue."

Welfare law is unyielding for the poor. But, like all other law, it can be bent or broken by government and business. A study made recently by the U.S. Department of Health, Education, and Welfare (HEW) showed that thirty-nine states are violating various federal laws and regulations in administering welfare programs. In most cases, by disregarding the law, the states are able to pay recipients less than they should, and HEW expects that it will take time to negotiate an end to these law violations. No court action is expected.

When a poor man breaks the law and is caught, the poor man goes to jail. A wealthy alcoholic found drunk on a public street or behind the wheel of a car is sent home, perhaps after posting collateral or paying a fine; the poor man shuffles through drunk court and off to a dirty cell. The professional criminal pays a bondsman to buy his freedom until trial; the poor man cannot afford bail and is locked up. Often, the white collar criminal who fixes prices, evades taxes, cheats his customers, or embezzles goes free after paying a fine; the poor man, a petty thief, more often is imprisoned. The man of means caught smoking marijuana, molesting a child, or beating his wife is generally sent away with a reprimand or allowed to enter voluntarily an expensive private institution; the poor man is virtually imprisoned in a crowded public hospital or is jailed. The rich man who drives recklessly without a license and leads police on a high-speed chase pays a stiff fine and goes home; the poor man is also given the same "$100 or fifty days" sentence, but he does not have $100, so he does the fifty days.

At every stage of a criminal proceeding, the poor man suffers from the same double standard of justice dispensed in the civil courts and by government agencies. The only difference is that second-class citizenship in criminal matters inevitably means jail. Our jails are our nation's punitive poor houses.

Because so many residents of our jails and so many defendants in our criminal courts are poor, because in recent years the public has become alarmed about rising crime, and because appellate courts have become increasingly concerned about the unequal lot of poor criminal defendants, steps *have* been taken to try to eliminate some inequities. All those charged with serious crimes must now be represented by lawyers, if necessary at no charge. Both the Bail Reform Act for federal courts and the experimental pretrial-release projects in many city and state courts have induced many judges to release without the posting of money bail defendants with local ties or steady jobs. In many places, the government will pay the cost of appeals of convictions and applications for writs of habeas corpus for poor defendants. Several recent Supreme Court decisions and other procedural changes in many courts make poor defendants more nearly legal equals to the state in criminal cases.

Unfortunately, most of the experiments fail to touch the majority of American criminal courts, and new requirements laid down by the Supreme Court are still widely ignored at the local level. Virtually nothing has yet been done about such relics of the debtor prison era as forcing a poor man convicted of even a minor traffic offense to work off a fine he cannot pay at the rate of a day in jail for every dollar or two of the fine imposed. More important, the assembly-line haste of most criminal courts today works against the rights of almost everyone, but especially against those of the poor defendant who cannot pay influential lawyers to make his case an exception. It would be foolish to argue that the poor man can find real justice in our criminal courts, where almost no one does.

Yet, criminal-law changes and recent court decisions do indicate at least an awakening recognition that the poor man is in theory the legal equal to anyone else. This is a step toward progress and a decided improvement over civil law, which still discriminates against poor people on its face as well as in its application. This is partly because nobody, until recently, has challenged the *status quo* on behalf of the poor, as lawyers have on behalf of Miranda, Mapp, and Gideon in the criminal field.*

"One reason why the content of the law of the poor permits broad, unchecked discretion," according to Carlin, "is

---

* In three decisions involving these criminal defendants, the U.S. Supreme Court greatly enlarged the legal rights of crime suspects, requiring that police warn them and help them get a lawyer after they are arrested (Miranda), protecting them from illegal searches by policemen (Mapp), and requiring that a lawyer be provided, free if necessary, for every defendant charged with a felony (Gideon).

because those subject to that law have not put it to the test of judicial review." For decades in the case of welfare assistance law and centuries in the case of tenant and debtor law, the supremacy of rich over poor and government over citizen has seldom been the issue of a court suit or an appeal.

Until recently, it was rare for a poor litigant even to have a lawyer with him in court. He could not pay for counsel in most cases, except for accident claims, in which he had to agree to pay a lawyer one third, one half, or more of whatever he won. Lawyers representing poor clients for contingency fees sought to win money settlements, not legal victories, in part because the client himself needed some money as soon as possible. Private practice lawyers turned down cases in which the law and courts discriminated the most against the poor—those involving tenant, debtor, and welfare rights—because no contingency fee was possible, and the poor could not otherwise pay.

Over the past two decades, the bar has responded to the need of the poor for legal help with the establishment of many new Legal Aid societies, financed by contributions from lawyers and such charity funds as the Community Chest and United Fund. In 1900, only New York and Chicago had Legal Aid offices: by 1948, there were still just fifty-five with paid staffs in the United States. Today, there are 600 offices, many of which, however, still depend on volunteers.

Legal Aid attorneys are generally overworked and underpaid in the extreme. Most earn less than $10,000 per year, many as little as $6,000 and $7,000. In big cities, each Legal Aid lawyer averages more than 1,000 cases each year, including about 200 court appearances. (Most private-practice attorneys handle no more than 100 cases each year and go to court only once or twice a week.) Legal Aid lawyers are so swamped with work that they must turn away many potential clients. Therefore, Legal Aid is loathe to advertise its existence, and the majority of the poor do not even know it exists. Few Legal Aid offices are located in the neighborhoods of the poor. Those clients Legal Aid lawyers do have the opportunity and time to see must be rushed through with quick interviews and encouraged to make some kind of out-of-court settlement with their adversaries.

Moreover, Legal Aid lawyers shy away from the meaningful legal confrontations with government or business that might enlarge the rights of the poor. They encourage their clients to pay their rent and meet contractual obligations or at least reach some compromise with a landlord or creditor. They never dare challenge rules or actions of government agencies, such as the welfare department. Only part of the reason for this is the overwhelming case load. Another determining factor is that the established bar, through direct contributions, and business, through charity funds, pay the bills for Legal Aid. Very seldom, if ever, do these groups approve of revolutionary assaults on the legal *status quo*. Legal Aid attorneys themselves also usually regard Legal Aid clients as charity cases, with no particular right to free legal help, who must go hat in hand to landlords, merchants, or government agencies and beg for some compromise of differences. Legal Aid attorneys have never helped their clients file for bankruptcy, for instance, because they did not believe they had that right. A rash of bankruptcies could reduce payment of creditors to a fraction of their claims, angering local merchants, with whom Legal Aid lawyers must bargain on behalf of other clients. Nor are Legal Aid lawyers anxious to upset their supporters in the bar by challenging the legal rights of creditors, who are the clients of influential lawyers. They also run the risk of increasing the work load of other lawyers by allowing the poor to file suit more often instead of compromising claims out of court.

Over the decades, the effect of this approach has been

to perpetuate the status of the poor as second-class citizens, unable to claim or exercise the same legal rights as everyone else. Only when a Legal Aid attorney would take his case could a poor man's legal problems receive any attention at all. But even then he was not given the same opportunity as other citizens to forgo compromise and fight for his rights in court. Even as Legal Aid lawyers were giving tirelessly of their meagerly remunerated time to advising poverty-stricken clients, they failed to take the much more important first step toward obtaining truly equal justice for the poor.

New Frontier legal advisers to Presidents John F. Kennedy and Lyndon Johnson, joined by leaders of the American Bar Association, who were insulated from the protectionist fears of local attorneys, recognized the shortcomings in legal help to the poor. When the federal "war on poverty" was proposed, they insisted that nothing of consequence could be done to improve the economic lot of the poor without considerably improving their legal standing. To do this, they proposed and won approval for the Legal Services projects of the Office of Economic Opportunity. In this program, the federal government was to finance enough lawyers to represent vast numbers of poor people with legal problems and take all cases to court when necessary. The lawyers were to be accessible and highly visible in neighborhood offices. They were to appeal lower-court decisions against the poor and launch test cases to enlarge the legal rights of the poor. With the kind of organizing advice and lobbying that high-priced lawyers provide large corporations and trade associations, the Legal Services lawyers were also supposed to help the poor obtain legal and political power in proportion to their share of the population.

The program's real *raison d'etre*, said its first national director, E. Clinton Bamberger, formerly an influential American Bar Association leader, was the "transfer of power to poor people." The Legal Services lawyers themselves called their mission "law reform."

By 1970, after a little more than a half decade of existence, the Legal Services projects funded by the federal government employed more than 2,000 lawyers in nearly 1,000 neighborhood storefront and mobile offices, in city ghettos and rural poverty areas. Even though the program has run into some trouble in the Nixon Administration, it has been the only OEO program to have its budget steadily increased. Its lawyers are helping more poor people fight creditors in court, obtain divorces, and declare bankruptcy than ever before. The attorneys are young, bright, and aggressive. Among them are many top graduates of leading law schools. They are motivated by the challenge facing them, rather than ambition for the high salaries and plush surroundings they might easily command.

Whereas some Legal Services lawyers have concentrated solely on individual cases and client needs, others have succeeded in modest efforts at law reform. In Washington, D.C., for example, these lawyers won the right for slum tenants not to be evicted when they stop paying rent if their landlords fail to keep up their housing. In several parts of the country, the federal and local governments were forced to ease some restrictions on welfare recipients, including one that had cut off aid to mothers of dependent children who have men living with them. In California and Florida, Legal Services lawyers helped organize Mexican-American migrant workers to fight low wages and poor working and housing conditions. In the Southwest, they have represented Indians in legal disagreements with government bureaucrats. In scattered local courts, they have managed to lower or eliminate some legal fees for the poor. In many places, they have fashioned out of the court suit a new weapon that some of the poor have been able to substitute for the political and financial leverage they lack to oppose arbitrary action by government in its administration of public housing, welfare, urban renewal, and other programs ostensibly designed to serve the poor.

One of the best examples of this new thrust is California Rural Legal Assistance (CRLA)—the epitome of what Bamberger envisioned in a Legal Services project. It was started by James Lorenz, son of a wealthy Dayton, Ohio, architect, high-honors graduate of Phillips Academy, Phi Beta Kappa at Harvard, *cum laude* graduate of Harvard Law, and new member of O'Melveny and Myers, the largest and most prestigious of Los Angeles's law firms. At twenty-eight, a man seemingly to be envied by all other young lawyers, he was dissatisfied. "I was just making more secure the people who already had security," he said.

After the Watts riots, he began asking questions about the poor in California. His interest moved from the poor of the city ghettos, newly discovered by the establishment because of the riots, to the still forgotten thousands of rural migrant workers, on whose bent backs the state's agricultural empire was built. "So far as the rural poor are concerned, the familiar saying that we are a society of laws, not of men, is at best a half truth," Lorenz wrote in his proposal to the OEO requesting federal money for the CRLA. "Laws are passed, interpreted and enforced by men; legal rights depend upon political, economic and legal representation. Yet this is what the rural poor, particularly the farm workers, have consistently lacked." As a remedy, he proposed not only to give the poor the legal aid that would equalize them with their economic superiors in court but also to upset the power structure and provide the poor with the legal capability that would truly enlarge their everyday rights.

The CRLA provided the necessary help for the efforts of Cesar Chavez to organize the grape workers. It convinced the Internal Revenue Service to simplify tax forms for

Spanish-speaking citizens. It went to court to force the U.S. Department of Agriculture to set up food benefit programs for 25,000 families in sixteen countries who had formerly been denied these programs and to win a ruling that Governor Ronald Reagan must rescind a cutback in medical services for 1.4 million state welfare recipients.

Other significant if somewhat less momentous victories have been won by other Legal Services projects. The success of Legal Services led to the inclusion of 700 lawyers in OEO's Volunteers in Service to America (VISTA) program. Instead of handling individual cases out of law offices, many VISTA lawyers began teaching the poor how to lobby with city housing, health, and welfare agencies to alter the way in which officials every day make discretionary decisions that deeply affect the poor but never receive legal review. In Washington, D.C., for instance, poor tenants and their VISTA lawyers pestered housing officials until they stopped issuing occupancy licenses to slum landlords whose buildings were unsafe or unsanitary.

But every small success on behalf of poor clients has created growing antagonism toward antipoverty lawyers from the entrenched interests they oppose and from the lawyers who make a living working for those interests. California's governor Ronald Reagan has tried again and again, for instance, to cut off financial support for the CRLA, which has been a constant thorn in his administration's side. Ex-Senator George Murphy of California, an outspoken friend of the grape and other growers there, sought to win congressional approval of an amendment that would have given governors, including Reagan, absolute power to veto those Legal Services projects that they did not want in their states. Only after a long struggle was it defeated. Governor Warren E. Hearnes, of Missouri, tried unsuccessfully to force the OEO to restrain Legal Services lawyers who organized rent strikes in crowded, dilapidated public housing in Saint Louis.

More recently, under the Nixon Administration, the OEO has begun to give ground to the critics of aggressive Legal Services projects. Lorenz, of the CRLA, for instance, was forced to agree that his lawyers would no longer represent Cesar Chavez's union as an entity in any proceeding. In 1969, the OEO approved reorganization of a Florida Legal Services project that had helped migrant citrus workers in a struggle with growers and the state for better working and living conditions. The project's supervisory board was changed to include among its eight members two picked by the citrus growers and three by former Republican Governor Claude Kirk, a critic of the project. The remaining three members were selected by the local bar association, which also was opposed to the young lawyers' activism, much of which was directed against wealthy clients of the established local bar.

By late 1970, OEO officials had agreed to give all local poverty officials—meaning, in many cases, governors or mayors or their representatives who were opposed to some Legal Services activities—a veto over what local Legal Services lawyers could or could not do. The Legal Services director at that time, Terry Lenzner, balked at this notion, and it was not made official policy, although Lenzner's aides complained that new "fine print" regulations for local projects went a long way toward accomplishing the same purpose. In November, Lenzner and his deputy were suddenly fired by OEO Director Donald Rumsfeld. Legal Services workers in the OEO and some American Bar Association leaders who had helped set up the program grew gloomy about its future in the law-reform field.

In many parts of the country, bar associations and influential lawyers have been rankled by the unprecedented challenges brought by Legal Services attorneys against established ways of doing things. The challenges threaten to prevent many of the easy victories won over the poor by the businessmen and their lawyers in the past, and they are forcing those lawyers and the local courts to deal with many more lawsuits from the poor than ever before.

Local bar associations have tried to intervene to curtail funding or dictate new policies for Legal Services programs in such cities as Albuquerque, New Mexico, Baton Rouge, Louisiana, Camden, New Jersey, Oklahoma City, Saint Louis, Missouri, and Washington, D.C. When Contra Costa County, California, was considering approval of a federal grant to a new Legal Services project there, an influential attorney warned the county supervisors that landlords, merchants, and taxpayers would be big losers if the antipoverty lawyers were allowed to bring suits for "trivial things" and erode creditors' rights.

But the alarmists are failing to notice that the balance has not really shifted very much, at least not yet. The progress made thus far by Legal Services lawyers, no matter how impressive it may appear when compared to the desolate past, adds up to little more than false hopes for the bulk of America's legally unequal poor. The new legal precedents established for poor litigants have come only in isolated cases in a comparatively few scattered jurisdictions. They have no effect on the way the law, courts, and government agencies deal with the poor in most of the nation. And, even in those cities and states where the test cases were won, the daily operation of courts and agencies often are unaffected by them. Local court judges in Washington, D.C., still evict tenants who fail to pay rent when the landlord is not maintaining his property, despite the appellate court decision to the contrary. Each case must be appealed separately for the precedent to be observed in many instances.

The vast majority of Legal Services offices across the country do not have sufficient personnel or time to try any test cases at all. They are too swamped with the problems of individual clients and too fearful of local bar opposition to engage in much, if any, law reform. Three lawyers in a Legal Services office in Los Angeles processed 5,800 cases in 1968 and 1969. If lawyers were to be made available to the poor in the same ratio as they are for the general population, Legal Services projects would have to hire 137,000 lawyers rather than the 2,000 now employed. The $60 million spent in 1971 by the federal government for Legal Services projects is the largest sum yet, but it is still a tiny fraction of the money spent by business and government to oppose the poor in court. Many Legal Services lawyers decline to put up with the long hours, low pay, and high pressure for more than a few years—and finally turn to private practice.

Some legal reformers have suggested that when landlords, creditors, and others lose cases to the poor they could pay the winners' legal expenses, which would expand the budgets of Legal Services projects. Some have proposed a "Judicare" program in which any qualifying poor person could choose any attorney at all and have his fee paid by the government. A few blue-chip law firms, such as the huge Piper and Marbury partnership in Baltimore, have opened public-service law offices in the ghetto and offer the services of their best newcomers free to the poor. Law reviews have argued that the poor have the same constitutional right to free counsel—by whatever means necessary—in civil cases that can deprive them of housing, jobs, or vital welfare benefits they do in criminal cases that can deprive them of their liberty.

But each suggestion appears to be severely limited in practicality at the moment by enormous costs (as in the case of Judicare), massive opposition by those who elect the lawmakers (including creditors and landlords who would have to pay the legal fees of the poor if they lost to them in court), or lack of assurance that expanded representation of the poor in civil cases would really change their relative position in court. Government programs that pay private-practice attorneys to represent the poor in criminal cases, for example, have not yet attracted high-quality lawyers to this work as a career. Much more remuneration than the government could ever pay will keep most lawyers on the side of the monied classes. Besides, putting out legal fires for the individual cases of poor clients in return for individual government stipends cannot be expected to promote systematic efforts to change laws, court rules, and government procedures that discriminate against the poor.

Judicare could mean more paternalistic legal aid. Lawyers would not be working for or with the poor as they do on retainer for monied clients or on salary from business or government. They would be doing relief work. There would be no reason for them to lobby for the poor, write new laws for the poor, or organize the poor into a potent political force. The poor would not be employing their own lawyers to direct their destiny and gain a stake in the community. Nothing would be done about the backlogs or inertia of trial courts and government agencies, which could brush off Judicare lawyers as easily as they now do Legal Services lawyers in most instances.

"The city agencies look upon you like a seven year plague: wait and suffer and it will go away," one discouraged Legal Services lawyer told an interviewer for an OEO evaluation study, cited by the Law Enforcement Task Force of the National Commission on the Causes and Prevention of Violence in *Law and Order Reconsidered*. He continued:

> They tell lawmakers and the budgetmakers plaintively how much money you cost them with your endless litigation over "hopeless cases" and small sums. The judges are worried about backlogs and court delay and cannot stifle their annoyance when we ask for jury trials in eviction cases, interpose eight defenses [none of them yet established at law] to the rent

[collection] action, file 25 *forma pauperia* divorce petitions in one week.

The appeals and test cases you hear so much about; they take so long. The test may be a success but the client has died, or been evicted, or moved away without his money. It takes over a year to get a case up to the Court of Appeals; our program has been going on for almost five years and we're just getting decided the cases the law professors were talking about back in 1964. The most basic kind of law reform will take decades in the courts; yet people think we have gotten it done already. An antitrust suit may drag on in the courts for five years with teams of full-time lawyers and millions poured into it; but a landlord-tenant victory that takes that long leaves everyone mad at you.

In this program you get used to having everyone mad at you. You seldom get to help your client in any basic way out of the interminable mess he lives in. You stay the eviction for one more week; get him a few more dollars on welfare, maybe keep the disturbed kid in his home a few months longer on probation before he gets in real trouble and is put away in training school. But so what, big deal. We don't get jobs for people; or build them houses; or give them real hope. We just take the edge off the "big lie." Like Demarol while your leg is being slowly amputated.

The sad truth these young lawyers discover is that American society, despite all its platitudes and promises, is still not ready to extend to the poor real economic help or real legal equality. Listen to Judge Charles W. Halleck, of the local Superior Court in Washington, D.C., complain that the law-reform test cases brought by Legal Services lawyers there are being used merely "to test novel legal points." Halleck has publicly derided the antipoverty attorneys as "crusading knights on white chargers [who] are trying to take every 15-cent case all the way up to the Supreme Court."

Another Washington judge, Milton Korman, finally told a

persistent Legal Services lawyer in court, "Your organization and everyone in it frightens me."

What appears really to frighten countless judges and lawyers throughout the nation is the prospect that Legal Services attorneys may actually achieve a measure of legal equality for the poor. It is not that the judges and the conventionally minded lawyers do not believe that the poor are entitled to fair treatment. Rather, they feel threatened, as does anyone who is comfortable with everything as it is now, by the revolutionary changes that must take place in our legal system, and in our society, before the poor are assured equal justice. But what they must face is that they are, in effect, defying the Constitution by standing in the way of today's urgent demands that the nation's legal hypocrisy, no matter how rooted in wrong-headed tradition, be ended now.

V

The Man in the Middle

For the middle-class American majority, the nation's legal system at first looks like ally and protector. For the most part, U.S. laws are written and amended by representatives of the middle class to preserve and safeguard middle-class values and interests; the personnel of the legal profession and the courts, who make the laws work, are largely from the middle class. As it has grown and prospered, the middle class in the United States has tended to identify itself more and more as a group that respects the law and gets a fair shake from it.

But that faith is being sorely tested these days—and frequently found wanting. Increasing numbers of middle-class citizens are coming into contact with the law, lawyers, and the courts. As often as not, they are disillusioned after ·f-fering nagging inconvenience, painful financial exploitation, or nightmarish catastrophe.

Consider these examples—some actual cases, others hypothetical but based on fact:

• A working man of middle-class means is driving through a city intersection when another car runs a red light and hits him. Hurt seriously in the collision, the man spends several weeks in the hospital, undergoes physical therapy for a year after that, and misses months of work. Through it all, he remains confident that the other driver's insurance, and the courts, assure him of repayment of the thousands of dollars he has spent in medical bills, plus lost income, and, perhaps, something extra to compensate him for the months of misery. But his trust is misplaced. More than likely, he will get back only half or even less of his out-of-pocket loss and nothing for his suffering. Worse, the chances are about one in twenty that he will end up being paid not one penny. If he insists on going to court to press his claim before a judge and jury in the big city where he lives, he will wait at least five years before his case comes to trial. If he has the patience and is fortunate enough to win his court suit eventually or a substantial settlement before trial, he must still give up anywhere from one third to one half or more of the money awarded him to pay his lawyer and court costs.

• A widow of comfortable means but no great wealth dies and leaves an estate worth a little more than $250,000. It takes three years for the case to go through the tortuous probate court labyrinth of paperwork and hearings. In the end, more than $120,000 is eaten up by fees for lawyers and executors and court costs. The heirs are left with little more than half of the original estate, *before* payment of death or inheritance taxes.

• A middle-class married couple reluctantly agrees to a divorce. They both want it to be as amicable and inexpensive as possible. Fortunately, they do not live in one of several states where it is still necessary for one or the other to trump up false adultery or cruelty charges, or to take a trip to Nevada or Mexico. But they still must hire lawyers, wait out a two-year legal separation, and endure months of court delays after that. When the filing of necessary papers and a brief court hearing are finally finished and the divorce completed, *each* will be left with a lawyer's bill for from

$1,000 to $2,000. They should still be thankful, however, that it is not a contested case, which would have doubled or tripled the attorneys' fees.

• Two working women from Queens who happen to witness a robbery during their lunch hour in Manhattan must wait in criminal court until nearly midnight for a suspect caught soon after the robbery to be processed by the judge. As it turns out, they are not called to testify. The policeman who volunteers to drive them home warns the women that they will probably be called back to court five or six more times as the case is shunted from courtroom to courtroom and date to date. Despite all the inconvenience and missed work, he adds, they may never have an opportunity to testify, because, in the vast majority of cases, the charge is dropped by the prosecutor or the defendant pleads guilty to a reduced charge.

• A man who gets a traffic ticket for an illegal turn believes he is a victim of a badly placed traffic sign and decides to have his case tried in court, rather than forfeit the $10 collateral he must post. He waits hours in crowded traffic court, losing a day at the office, only to be rushed through a two-minute hearing before the judge. The policeman's routine testimony prevails, and the harried judge, after remonstrating with the motorist for taking up the court's time, orders him to pay a $25 fine.

• A family buying a new $35,000 suburban home is told by the real-estate broker that the law requires that a lawyer draw up the necessary papers, hold the money, and perform the closing settlement of the sale. The family goes to the title attorney recommended by the broker, makes the agreed down payment in cash, obtains a mortgage loan from a bank for the balance, signs the papers, and moves into the house. Several months later, it finds it does not own its home after all. The title lawyer, it turns out, has used the money for something else. He never paid off the old liens on the house or completed the sale. The family must now pay off the old liens, in addition to its own mortgage, or lose its home.

• A middle-class black family that has just moved to a comfortable old house beyond the fringe of the big-city ghetto is persuaded by a home improvement salesman to have a new roof, aluminum siding, and shutters put on the house. The job is botched, and the contractor uses materials inferior to those promised. The final price, with added financing charges, is much higher than expected. The homeowner decides not to pay until the work is done properly and the price adjusted, and he so informs the home improvement firm. He hears nothing more about it until he is warned by a letter from a finance company that his house will be auctioned off at a foreclosure sale if he does not pay the home improvement debt. The finance company had bought, from the home improvement firm, the homeowner's promissory note and a mortgage on his house securing it. The homeowner then turns to a lawyer for help but is told he has little choice but to pay or lose his house. Proving fraud on the part of the home improvement firm would be difficult under the law, the lawyer explains, and succeeding in doing it might still not alter the legal right of the finance company to collect on the note it now owns. Besides, the attorney adds, any court fight probably would cost more in legal fees than the amount of the home improvement note and would last a year or two, or longer.

Thus it is that middle-class citizens—who have only lately begun to learn that their laws and courts systematically discriminate against the poor—are discovering each day that the cold legal bureaucracy can be indifferent to them, too, that a large group of lawyers feed as parasites on the backs of the middle class, and that chaos and delay in the courts, along with the high cost of legal representation, can make justice seem an insurmountable mountaintop.

Daily, they are thrown into the presence of lawyers and courts by the legal requirements for divorce, probate, and the transfer of home ownership, by their civic duty when called as witnesses or jurors, by the numerous calamities that can occur when driving a car, or through economic victimization. As litigants, witnesses, jurors, and traffic defendants, middle-class citizens are the courts' most numerous clients. Today, they may also be the most thoroughly neglected.

The landed rich and the captains of industry have always been able to buy the best legal representation. Often, they also can negotiate their way to favorable legal settlements without even stepping into the maelstrom of the courts. They can pay their lawyers to wait, or even to prolong the law's normal delay until they wear down opponents with fewer resources. The lawyers for the rich and the big corporations work on a fixed retainer fee that is paid no matter what kind of case they handle, so long as they maintain strong allegiance to their client.

However belatedly, the poor in many parts of the nation now are also being furnished "house counsel" of their own: teams of government-paid poverty lawyers and salaried volunteers from private law firms, many of them bright recent law school graduates who, for a few years at least, prefer public service to larger fees. Not only are these young champions winning court battles the poor had been accustomed to losing, but they also are imitating high-priced lawyers and short-circuiting the overloaded court system to redress grievances with determined legal negotiation. Like the rich, who can easily afford it, the poor who qualify need not worry about counsel fees; they do not have to pay them. Like the rich man's attorneys, poverty lawyers need not worry about rationing their time in proportion to fees, because they are paid the same for every client and every case.

All this leaves the middle-class citizen uncomfortably neglected. Too poor to put a lawyer to work for him whenever he wishes and for as long as necessary, and too affluent to qualify for free legal assistance, he is finding that he cannot always turn to a lawyer when he thinks he needs one. When legal advice is required whether he wants it or not, financial crisis threatens. The high cost of legal representation and the long delays in legal proceedings today are the enemies of justice for the middle-class citizen. He must choose between compromising his claim early in the game and risking still more legal expense for the chance at victory in the end.

The lawyers' answer to the dilemma is the "contingent fee" in cases in which the client is suing for money damages. If the litigant loses, his lawyer charges nothing. But, if his client wins, the lawyer qualifies by prior agreement for one third to one half or more of his winnings. In this arrangement, the middle-class litigant must accept the lawyer as his financial partner and stand aside as the attorney adds self-interest or substitutes it for the interest of his client. Another result is that few attorneys will force other attorneys to lose out entirely; after all, it could happen to them, too. Most frequently, then, opposing attorneys compromise their causes. Each collects fees from the funds of others. So, for the middle-class litigant, half a loaf must often suffice.

The court system, which forces the middle-class citizen to pay so dearly when he makes use of it, returns him very little when he is called to serve it. Witnesses in criminal cases are paid a minimum of $4 or $5 per day in many courts and seldom more than $10. Court officials often do not even tell witnesses that they are eligible for compensation, according to a study made in 1966 by the President's Commission on Law Enforcement and the Administration of Justice.

Jurors in most jurisdictions are paid between $10 and $20 per day, and they are paid even less in some.

The low compensation is a hardship for many working men paid by the hour, day, or week whose employers do not pay them for days they are serving as witnesses or jurors. In Washington, D.C., for instance, a $40-a-day truck-driver with six children lost $574 in wages during a recent year when he was called sixteen times to appear as a witness in a criminal case and was reimbursed only $4 for each day by the government.

Just as disturbing to people who, despite the financial hardship, do their duty as witnesses and jurors is the rudeness with which they are treated in court. Waiting facilities are crowded and dirty or do not exist at all. Jurors called to serve from a week to a month of duty are often shuffled about to be ready for this case or that, only to spend most of their time waiting for trial duty that never comes. A journalist called as a juror recently complained about the feeling that he was being "manipulated, used, and otherwise treated as a pawn in a game."

Witnesses in criminal cases are forced to return to court again and again without ever testifying, as their case is repeatedly postponed and then finally disposed of without a trial. Those witnesses who actually were the victims of the crimes at issue find little solace or justice in this treatment. Others, the bystanders who chose this once, in the interest of justice, to become involved, are actively discouraged from doing so again. In characteristic lawyer-like understatement, a former New York prosecutor warned the President's Crime Commission that "complainants and witnesses are innocent victims in these situations, and some real thought should be given as to how to minimize the inconvenience . . . and to make them feel that what they are doing is appreciated by the people and the authorities."

As he chafes under the delays and the bureaucratic indifference and as he witnesses the chaos and the mass processing of cases, the middle-class citizen serving as a witness or juror both experiences and views injustice. The memory of his experience is bound to jaundice his view of his nation's courts.

Much the same kind of disillusionment can be expected inside another portal through which the middle class frequently enters into contact with the legal system—traffic court.

In most jurisdictions, not everyone who runs afoul of the traffic laws need go to court. Collateral, which must be posted to remain free from arrest until the trial date, can simply be forfeited as an admission of guilt. Perhaps three fourths of all moving-traffic violations are disposed of this way. But motorists who believe that they are in the right, who hope the court fine will be less than the collateral deposit, or who want the judge to keep the penalty points from this latest offense off their record so that their licenses will not be suspended (as they now are in many jurisdictions after a certain number of points from ⁻convictions accumulate) exercise their right to come to court to be heard.

What they find are some of the most crowded courtrooms in America, with the most dehumanizingly mechanical methods for sweeping the horde through quickly. In many traffic courts, several defendants are processed at once, with only those doggedly insisting on a separate hearing getting one, and that coming after everyone else is disposed of. "Trials" are usually two- to five-minute hearings dominated by sketchy police testimony. Cross-examination of the policemen and other time-consuming tactics are discouraged by the judges.

In many cities, traffic court defendants never have lawyers. Nor are many of the trappings of constitutional due process observed. Legal rights are seldom explained. In some traffic courts, witnesses are not even sworn. In Los Angeles, traffic defendants are crowded into a room seating about two hundred people and brought before the judge row by row. In Cleveland, traffic court is located in a run-down makeshift courtroom in the old police headquarters building, where most of the processing is handled by a policeman-bailiff standing in the middle of a milling crowd of bewildered defendants. He sorts out their cases, sends those who plead guilty off to pay their fines, and takes the rest up before the judge.

In a few places, including New York City and Washington, D.C., some lawyers regularly wait around traffic court to solicit prospective clients in the hall outside. These traffic court hangers-on find citizens with tickets who are fearful that another violation conviction will mean suspension of their license. With a door-to-door salesman's delivery, they convince them that they need a lawyer's help, making it appear that they know some secret about solving the confusion of traffic court and winning more than a perfunctory hearing for their clients.

"You here on a traffic case?" a lawyer in a rumpled suit, carrying a small datebook in his hand, asked an obviously confused man outside the traffic courtroom in New York's teeming Criminal Court Building. "That judge in there today is a tough one." He eased the man into a quiet corner in the hall. "Let me help you out."

In fact, most of these lawyers do very little to help their quickly solicited clients. The defendant usually is rushed through a short hearing, and often the lawyer fails even to stand beside him. In each case, the lawyer has already collected his cash fee (whatever he could talk the citizen out of) in advance in the corridor outside.

However, some traffic court specialists do appear to work minor miracles for their clients, gaining in the process a courthouse reputation that increases the volume of their

customers and the size of their fees. These victories are
seldom won in traffic court itself on the merits of the cases,
however, but rather in contacts between the lawyers and
the city solicitors who prosecute the traffic cases. The result
is dropped charges or, in cities where they are permitted,
agreements to send violators to "traffic school" rather than
convict them and suspend their licenses. These lawyers
sometimes charge several hundred dollars for their brief service to a middle-class client.

"That is often what it is worth to a man who can afford it
to keep his driver's license," explains one young Washington,
D.C., lawyer, who claims to earn $20,000 or more each year
from "hustling" traffic cases in the local Court of General
Sessions. "I've charged as much as $500 to $1,000 for particularly difficult cases when the client was able to afford it,"
he says. "Mostly though, I get $50 to $100 for a few minutes' work."

In parts of the country through which middle-class tour-
ists in automobiles pass in large numbers on vacations, the
profit in traffic court goes instead to officials of crossroads
towns. Out-of-state motorists caught speeding are rushed
before the local mayor or magistrate operating as judge in
a makeshift traffic court and are fined heavily for their
transgressions. Failure to pay often means jail until the
money can be secured from home. A recent American Bar
Association study of small-town and rural traffic courts in
Florida showed that many of these "judges" were nonlaw-
yers and received a part of the traffic fines as their fee. Some
of the towns in which they serve derive most of their municipal revenues from traffic fines. In some parts of Florida,
the study noted, policemen frequently collect the fines from
the motorists right on the roadway as they stop them for
violations.

The result of all this is that, in most jurisdictions, traffic
court is devoid of legal purpose and of justice. If its purpose

were to provide a judicial determination of disputed traffic violations, treating them as criminal-court cases, traffic court would have to provide sufficient due process or decorum to make that possible. If its purpose were to improve driver safety by impressing traffic violators with the gravity of their error and the concern of the government, something would have to be done about the pointless hubbub and bureaucratic haste that greet violators in court. As it is, the vast majority of violators avoid traffic court altogether, by forfeiting the collateral they must post after being ticketed.

There seems to be little reason why traffic courts should not be abolished and replaced by closely supervised arms of state or city motor-vehicle agencies that would simply collect fixed fines from violators and provide administrative hearings for those who wish to contest the citation. These agencies already handle auto registration and the licensing of drivers, and this new function would be a logical extension of those responsibilities. (Philadelphia and recently New York have experimented with variations of this idea.) Criminal traffic violations—homicide, reckless driving that causes serious injury, leaving the scene of an accident, and perhaps drunk driving—could be treated as criminal charges to be processed through the criminal courts with full due process and the threat of imprisonment on conviction. But the present possibility of a man's being jailed for failure to pay a $25 ticket for an illegal turn or for slightly exceeding the speed limit is an injustice; converting a court of law into a money-making scheme is a perversion of legal process. Traffic court itself is chaotic and pointless, draining unnecessarily the resources of the parent court system.

But, if traffic court involves the middle-class citizen in a shabby back room of the court system, then another legal by-product of the age of the automobile—the personal-injury suit—takes him into the main hall itself. There he finds himself even more bewildered and threatened with much greater injustice.

Each year in the United States, there are about 15 million traffic accidents. According to statistics, every driver will probably be involved, in his lifetime, in at least one accident. The total cost of the annual highway holocaust in terms of damage to property and injury to persons is something more than $10 billion each year, about half of that being medical bills and lost wages for injury victims. The majority of the victims are, of course, middle-class citizens, who do the most driving.

People who damage their own cars or hurt themselves in one-car accidents usually pay for it themselves or collect on their own collision insurance. Any time two or more cars crash, however, or, when a car hits a pedestrian, it is a potential law case. In fact, auto accident cases, particularly those involving bodily injury, are the single largest source of business and income for the legal community.

The reason is a common-law tradition, which dates from long before the automobile or the birth of the United States and which decrees that the person at fault in an accident should compensate the innocent victim. To protect against the day that they may be adjudged to have caused someone else injury, most drivers buy liability insurance, and the insurance to which company they have been paying premiums will pay what they owe to the victim of their negligence. Such insurance would seem to make sense: Innocent accident victims are compensated for their loss, with the wrongdoer or his insurer righting the wrong.

But, in reality, it seldom works out that way. In the vast majority of cases, there are disagreements about who is at fault or how great a financial loss the victim has suffered. These disagreements are most often between the victim and the insurance company for the other driver. Sometimes, they compromise their differences. But, in millions of cases each year, an injured auto accident victim turns to a lawyer, or is contacted by one seeking out accident cases, and enters the legal system for help.

These legal disputes, known as personal injury (PI in the trade) or negligence cases, take up four-fifths of the time and resources of our civil courts. More than 200,000 auto negligence cases are filed each year in New York City alone. Fees that lawyers take in from handling these cases account for one-fourth to one-half of the legal profession's aggregate income each year, according to the best estimates. Thousands of negligence specialists do nothing else, and almost every lawyer in private practice has at least a few PI cases in his briefcase at any given moment.

But all this time and expense for the legal system fails to achieve full justice in a majority of cases. Studies made in several states show that more than half of the auto accident victims who appeal to the legal system wind up being reimbursed for less than half of their out-of-pocket medical expenses and wage losses. And from one to three of every twenty victims, according to the various studies, receives nothing at all from his negligence claim. A majority of the accident victims who become PI cases and pursue claims against other drivers for their injuries do not get satisfaction but suffer instead painful out-of-pocket losses.

Why? It is, of course, often difficult to prove that the other driver was negligent. More often, however, the other driver is clearly at fault, but the victim, too, is found to have been negligent to some extent. And, if there is the slightest evidence of negligence by the victim, the law does not allow him to collect, no matter how reckless the other driver was. This is called the rule of "contributory negligence." Most states use such a rule. In almost every other nation, however, a "comparative negligence" rule is used, meaning that a partially negligent victim is still awarded damages, but proportionately less in relation to his negligence.

According to the studies, even if the victim has an airtight case, however, he must wait an average of from three to six or more years before he can go before a judge and jury to win his claim. Auto negligence cases are the biggest source of delay in our civil courts. The most tangled cases last as long as ten years in cities like Chicago, New York, and Philadelphia and, in turn, of course, create horrendous delays in the rest of the courts' work.

Sometimes, the delay is caused deliberately by the lawyer for the sued driver's insurance company because the victim frequently cannot wait several years for a trial; he has bills to pay now. But the other driver's insurance company, and its lawyers, are in no hurry. They offer the victim the option of enduring the long wait for trial or accepting a settlement for much less than he is seeking. The victim often gives in and agrees to a settlement for substantially less than the loss he actually suffered. As Maryland lawyer Jack H. Olender wrote in the *Young Lawyer* magazine of the American Bar Association, to win even this much, the victim's lawyer must be "a salesman. He has a product to sell—the injuries and their concomitant expenses, pain and suffering, loss of income, etc. If he is to obtain optimal results, he must, like any other salesman, demonstrate to the prospective buyer that the purchase is advantageous."

In practice, a lawyer who deals frequently with the same lawyers and claims adjusters for an insurance company also will compromise on one victim's claim to get more money for another. "I gave in a thousand on Jones," goes the standard bargaining ploy. "You come up a thousand on Smith."

Is this the law at work? Is this justice? Even when trials are held, the law means little. Most auto negligence trials are merely swearing contests between witnesses for the two sides.

The accident itself was a split-second event that occurred years before and that can no longer be remembered clearly by any of the participants or witnesses. On the question of who was negligent and how much loss the victim has suffered, there is much more perjury by witnesses than judges or lawyers admit in public. The victim's lawyer often is preoccupied by his client's appearance to the jury: Does he look honest? Does he appear to have suffered? Some lawyers have their secretaries take notes on each client's appearance during pretrial interviews so that supposed defects, such as peroxided hair or an offensive manner, can be corrected. Even so, because of the contributory negligence rule and because insurance companies, before trial, settle cases they are certain to lose, the victims who go to trial wind up approximately half the time losing and get nothing.

The victim who wins a large award after trial or a large settlement before must give up as much as half or more to pay attorney fees and court costs. Under the standard contingent fee contract—and lawyers will seldom take auto negligence cases without such a contract—the lawyer gets 33 per cent to 50 per cent, and more often the latter. The only limit is the percentage the client agrees to in advance. In this way, the legal profession takes in between $1 billion and $2 billion each year, and, whereas the client frequently loses, relative to the loss he actually suffered, his lawyer always wins. And, of course, the client must also pay court costs, stenographers' fees, and the like. The lawyer is not being paid in relation to actual work done on each case. He is entitled to his agreed percentage of the winnings whether he pilots the case through an arduous trial or wins a quick settlement, whether the award is for everything the victim suffered in financial loss or covers less than half of it, whether it is $1,000 or $100,000. In practice, the lawyer has become a partner in his client's lawsuit.

Defenders of the contingent fee system say that it is the

only way many litigants, even from the middle class, could afford a lawyer for these cases. The lawyers are also free to take less than the agreed percentage, and sometimes they do. But, because of the obvious evils, the contingency fee is illegal throughout most of the world—except for the United States, Spain, and a single Canadian province.

The prospect of a big windfall fee has converted many lawyers into "ambulance chasers," who go from accident to accident, or have runners who do, looking for victims who appear likely to win big claims. They then take on the victims as clients or refer them to other negligence case specialists, in return for a share of the specialist's fee. Some lawyers make their livings solely on such referral fees. These practices violate lawyers canons of ethics but are nonetheless widespread.

Of course, many accident victims finally do get back more than they actually suffered in losses. But their cases only underscore the inequities and injustice of the negligence law system. Many of them are persons with claims of less than $1,000 who are paid handsomely and quickly by the opposing insurance company to avoid a drawn-out case that would cost more in expenses than the settlement. In some small cases, insurance company lawyers are also inclined to be a little more generous in settlements to assure their opposite members of sufficiently large contingency fees. Some victims and lawyers succeed in parlaying exaggerated or even fictitious claims of "pain and suffering" into overly generous settlements or jury awards. Still other victims collect, in addition to their award from the negligence case, claims on health-loss and wage-loss insurance policies or group plans. Although, taken together, the instances of overpayment are a marked minority of negligence cases, they do reduce the amount of compensation available for other accident victims and substantially raise the cost of auto liability insurance. "Only the lawyers have profited continually and without exception" from the negligence law system, legal journalist Murray Teigh Bloom has written.

There have been many suggestions for change, such as speeding up court processing of negligence cases by setting deadlines for various legal moves, holding pretrial hearings and settlement conferences with judges, and the like. Those suggestions that have been acted on have been found wanting as long-range solutions to delay and have done nothing to alter other inequities in the system. For example, Arkansas has been testing, since the mid-1950's, a change from the contributory negligence rule to one of comparative negligence, therefore allowing a victim who was also negligent to recover *some* money, rather than none at all. Studies show that the experiment has somewhat increased the equitability of settlements, but it has not reduced court delays or congestion. An American Bar Association committee has recommended that comparative negligence be the rule in all courts, but few states (probably because of insurance company opposition) are rushing to adopt it.

Several changes in the system of liability insurance have also been proposed. A study team from the University of Pennsylvania Law School's Institute of Legal Research has suggested that a new kind of insurance be available for an accident victim to collect on when his own collision insurance, the other driver's liability insurance, and the court system fail to make up more than a small fraction of the victim's accident loss. This would, of course, mean more insurance premiums to pay and would do nothing to abate the chaos of the present system on top of which the new insurance would be placed.

Harvard law professor Robert E. Keeton and a colleague from the University of Illinois, Jeffrey O'Connell, in their book *After Cars Crash*, have proposed a widely publicized new insurance system that would pay an accident victim a limited amount of money to compensate for medical bills and wage loss, irrespective of who was at fault in the accident. In 1970, Massachusetts became the first state to try this system. Each driver is required to buy his own no-fault "basic protection" insurance policy to provide such coverage. Collision insurance would still indemnify drivers against damage done to their cars. This scheme would eliminate legal quarreling over fault in the majority of accidents, in which losses from injuries to the parties involved do not exceed several hundred dollars each. But, for larger claims and for additional compensation for "pain and suffering" (a very real loss to thousands of accident victims each year), the victim would still have to go to court to sue the other driver. For those hundreds of thousands of cases, the system would not be changed, except that each victim could collect on the limited no-fault basic protection coverage while awaiting the outcome of his court case.

A plan put before the New York state legislature by Governor Nelson Rockefeller and his insurance commissioner, Richard E. Stewart, would go further, very nearly eliminating the question of fault and entirely abolishing the negligence legal system. In this plan, each driver would buy enough insurance to cover all loss arising from damage to his car, injury to himself and anyone else in his car, and damage to any object or person struck by his car (except another automobile and its contents), in any accident, no matter who was at fault.

In a collision, the driver and occupants of one car would be covered by that driver's insurance; the driver and occupants of a second car would be covered by the insurance of the second driver. Actual loss in auto repairs, medical bills, and wages would be paid. Only in cases of claimed "pain and suffering" beyond that limit would an accident victim proceed against another driver. Stewart insists that his plan, because of enormous savings in administrative and legal costs, would actually cut premium rates even though victims would recover more money than they have heretofore. Because only actual loss would be compensated and the money recovered from other insurance would be deducted first, there would be no more overpayment. Stewart has estimated that, in New York, only about 15 cents of every insurance-premium dollar goes to repay the actual money losses of accident victims. The rest goes to insurance-company administrative and sales expenses (33 cents), lawyers and claims adjusters (23 cents), and "pain and suffering" awards (21 cents).

Stewart's is the most sweeping reform proposal made thus far. Insurance companies are afraid of such a drastic change in the way they do business. Lawyers are fighting the proposal because they fear it will dry up their primary source of fee income. Lawyers have also fought the more limited Keeton-O'Connell no-fault plan—introduced in many legislatures but passed only in Massachusetts—for the same reason, even though it appears that lawyers would still be left with plenty of work under that plan. A note of warning on the political future of these reform proposals: The majority of state legislators are lawyers, as are the majority of the local city, town, and courthouse political leaders who help put them into office.

Of course, even under the Stewart plan, disagreements could arise between a victim and his own insurance company over the dollar value of his out-of-pocket losses. Stewart contemplates continuation of a *laissez faire* legal marketplace in which these victims would hire lawyers and pay them whatever is agreed on as a fee. This fee could be paid by the insurance company if the claimant prevails in the disagreement. The lawyer's fees could be limited to a certain percentage by law, as they now are for lawyers representing claimants seeking increases in awards from workmen's compensation boards. The real tests for Stewart's plan, if it were to win the uphill fight for legislative approval, would be

whether lawyers find a way to push their way in and knock
the plan's economic calculations off kilter, and whether,
even without the intrusion of lawyers, it lowers insurance
costs the way its author predicts.

Although a change in the auto-negligence system could
make a large difference for accident victims and do much
to reduce court backlogs, another growing negligence law
field would still be left untouched—consumer recovery of
damages from makers or sellers of faulty, dangerous, or
shoddy goods and services. The increasing use of new drugs
and appliances, not to mention automobiles themselves,
has multiplied the number of consumers suffering losses
from faulty products and, as a result, the number who turn
to lawyers and the courts.

Until very recently, most legal complaints of this type
were simply turned away with a *caveat emptor:* Unless the
maker or seller had given a written warranty against the
specified fault found with the product, the buyer had only
himself to blame and could not recover legal damages.
Lately, however, many more judges than before are ruling
that defects built into automobiles and harmful side effects
of new drugs, which the maker either knew or should have
found out about before marketing the product, are cause for
awarding proven victims of the dangerous products compensation from the maker.

There are still too few precedents, however, to say that
the consumer is now assured of legal protection against
built-in product defects. Each case is, in effect, a test case of
how far the judge will go. Must the victim prove in every
case that the maker knew or should have known about the
defect? Is the seller also liable? What about a product that
does not work but is not dangerous and does not cause the
buyer any loss except his wasted purchase price? Can he

win a complaint on that ground, too, and recover what he paid?

More important, to take this kind of case to court is just as expensive as an automobile accident liability claim. Those who win in court must pay out as much as half or more of their awards for legal fees. What many consumer advocates seek now is legislation that would allow a few victims of widespread product defects or consumer frauds to sue in the name of everyone so victimized. If such litigation, called "class action," succeeded in proving the consumers' case, then every other person who suffered the same way could also recover without proving the whole case all over again. This can now be done in some cases in court if and when a judge can be persuaded to rule that a particular suit qualifies as a class action—something that seldom happens because of unclear legal precedents. Business interests, as might be expected, are fighting hard against congressional enactment of this legislation.

Finally, there is the radical notion being championed by a few lawyers that business and government should also be prevented from carrying on activities that harm all of society—such as smokestack emissions that pollute the air—even though no single citizen may be able to prove how he in particular has suffered. In one test case, conservationists won a court order forbidding the laying of an oil pipeline from Alaska that, they argued, would harm Arctic flora and fauna. In this area, too, the legal arguments are novel and must be tested by years of litigation. That process is expensive, and many litigants discouraged by the cost and long waits give up.

Court delays and lawyers' fees, plus a third factor—seemingly discriminatory laws—combine to treat the middle class unfairly when they are forced into court by another kind of catastrophe: an unworkable marriage. Today, roughly one of every three marriages ends in divorce. There is a growing body of opinion that if a husband and wife cannot live harmoniously together, it may be best for them, and for any children they may have, if they can be divorced with as little destructive bitterness and legal fighting as possible.

Such an outcome is difficult to achieve in states where adultery or cruelty must be proved, where a spouse who does not want a divorce can block it interminably in the courts, where the laws open the way for battles over alimony and property division, and where long separation periods, usually two years or more, are required. Under these circumstances, only the rich can end their marriages easily, by, for example, establishing residence for six weeks in Nevada or a month in the Caribbean. Middle-class partners agreeing on a divorce often must invent disputes or infidelities to qualify under their states' laws. Those involved in contested divorces must endure emotionally and financially debilitating court battles. For some, the easiest method has been permanent separation without the legal finality of a divorce.

New York, in 1967, did away with an archaic divorce law that previously allowed dissolution of marriage only on the grounds of adultery. Couples there can now win uncontested divorces after two years' voluntary separation. California went further in 1969 and allowed divorce for any reason whatsoever with the only requirement being six months' residency in the state. Arguments about adultery or alimony are not allowed. Community property is divided evenly. Neither state, however, has taken the ultimate—and financially most important—step and eliminated the need for lawyers in uncontested divorce cases. In both places, attorneys are still necessary, as in every other state, to file the papers and represent each spouse in the brief court hearing. Why? Probably because lawyers wrote the divorce reform laws and made certain that the profession did not lose a lucrative source of income. For tasks that could be carried out by a layman—filling out papers, taking them to court, and talking to a judge about a matter not involving legal expertise—lawyers still collect fees averaging $1,000 and $2,000 for uncontested divorce cases in New York and California, as in many other states. Lawyers in Connecticut, for instance, often base their fees for middle-class divorce clients on a percentage of the money and property to be divided.

The enrichment of lawyers in divorce proceedings has another source noted in the widely reported efforts of many divorce lawyers to convince a spouse seeking an amicable settlement that he or she could do better in the financial arrangements being agreed to. A fight over this, of course, delays the settlement of the case, runs up the lawyer's fee, and contributes to the trauma associated with the divorce.

Only California now makes this sort of ploy impossible by eliminating alimony and forcing an even division of community property, no matter what the circumstances. Not everyone welcomed the change. "I'm a little old-fashioned about it," one divorce lawyer in California was quoted as saying after the new law was passed there. "I don't think that a wife, or husband, who takes up residence with another of the opposite sex should still be entitled to half the community property."

Another middle-class legal field in which the law allows lawyers to take large fees for work many laymen could do for themselves is probate. When the estate of a dead person is distributed to his heirs, the process must be supervised by a court—a probate court in most states. Although the average middle-class estate is devoid of legal controversy or financial complications, it is still necessary under many state laws for a lawyer to guide the estate through probate court. Often, this means little more than the filing of various kinds of papers. The paper work is more complicated than that for divorce cases, but only because nobody has taken the trouble to streamline unnecessarily complicated, archaic procedures that now require years for each probate case.

Lawyers get into the picture when they are named by the deceased in his will as executor or when the law requires that one must be hired by a lay person or a bank named as executor. Often, a lawyer named as executor hires *another* lawyer to represent him in the probate proceedings. In many places, the law requires him to. Other lawyers are hired additionally to represent and protect the interests of minor heirs as legal guardians for the duration of the probate process. The resulting legal fees mount up quickly, to an estimated national total of $500 million each year. The executor is usually entitled by law or custom to a fixed percentage—no matter how much work is required—of the estate's total value, up to 10 per cent for medium-sized estates in many states, with the allowable percentage, for very large estates, lower, but, of course, the dollar amount higher. The executor's attorney, in many jurisdictions, is entitled to a fee half that of the executor. Each can earn still more if there is extraordinary litigation—in a dispute among heirs, for instance—and the judge approves a larger fee. Lawyer-guardians for minor children can take whatever the court will allow out of the estates. Standard practice is to charge from $50 to $100 and more per hour for such work as telephoning to make certain there are no other heirs, checking the minor's birth certificate, and thinking about whether his rights are being observed in the proceeding. Often, lawyer-guardians submit bills for 100 hours or more in the preparation of a short report to the court certifying that the minor's rights were protected.

These guardians are appointed by the court, and the pattern of appointments has been a frequent cause of scandal in those places where elected probate judges hand lucrative guardian appointments to political cronies. New York City's

Surrogate (probate) Court has periodically been a source of this kind of problem, and the practice never seems to stop.

Even legitimate costs for lawyer and court take about one dollar in five out of each estate probated. It is not unusual for an estate of $100,000 (a middle-class man's not infrequent legacy to his wife and children) to be cut in half by the expenses of probate.

Beyond this, in state after state, the records of legal disciplinary bodies are full of complaints that lawyers serving as executors have converted large amounts of the estate's money to their own use during the years of probate court delays. Such practice is one of the most frequent causes for lawyer disbarment. These "improper practices" (as the *Journal of the American Bar Association* has labeled them) and high costs of probate are not loudly disputed by the bar these days. Much publicity has been given to scores of shocking examples in the press and in such books as Norman F. Dacey's *How to Avoid Probate* and Murray Teigh Bloom's *The Trouble With Lawyers*. The *ABA Journal* has in fact warned lawyers that, although many of Dacey's points can be disputed, it is time for the bar "to take to heart the criticisms that have been aimed at lawyers" in the probate field. Among themselves, however, lawyers still envy each other's big probate cases, still the surest and easiest road to big fees. Every lawyer, no matter what his specialty, tries to keep some on hand at all times.

Just as some laymen who have tried to dispense with lawyers and probate the estate of a relative or friend by themselves are told they must hire and pay a lawyer whether they need one for the actual work involved or not, so, others, when buying a house, are required, in many states, to hire lawyers to fill out and file forms. Laws in those states forbid those who buy or sell a home, or even licensed real estate brokers, to write contracts and deeds for real property, or to perform the "settlement," when money and deed actually change hands. Lawyers who specialize in this are called title attorneys, and efforts to sidestep them and complete real estate transactions without a lawyer have drawn opposition from bar committees on the "unauthorized practice of law." Whenever the question has gone to court, the lawyers have won: Both seller and buyer must have attorneys, or a neutral title attorney must be used for settlement, depending on the state. This practice adds hundreds of dollars to the cost of buying a house.

Of course, it would seem advantageous for an unsophisticated buyer who could afford it to have an attorney looking out for his interests in the purchase of a $40,000 house and the financial obligations that go along with it. The problem is that title attorneys sometimes cannot be trusted. Three title attorneys were sent to prison in Maryland in 1967 after it was discovered that they had spent money given them by home buyers to hold. The buyers were legally required to pay their down payment and turn their mortgage loan over to the title attorneys, who were then supposed to pay the seller or builder of the house and satisfy any old liens. These lawyers pocketed the money instead, and, months after moving in under the assumption that they had bought their houses, dozens of families were told they did not have clear title and owed old liens that the title attorneys had not paid off. When the Maryland General Assembly set about changing the law to stop that from happening again, the title lawyers successfully lobbied against legislation that would require them to put the money in untouchable escrow bank accounts, have themselves bonded, or make public accountings of their finances.

In all of the many kinds of situations cited in this chapter, the middle-class citizen often finds that the law will not work for him when he needs it. Instead, the law is used by others arbitrarily to deny him justice. A frequent, heart-breaking example is the way some merchants use the law to force customers to pay for shoddy merchandise and workmanship or disputed bills. Also, the middle-class homeowner is the frequent unsuspecting victim of home improvement specialists, including many large, otherwise reputable merchandising firms, that frequently require homeowners to sign mortgages on their homes to secure large bills for remodeling. Fly-by-night con artists also get many a homeowner's signature on a mortgage, usually without his knowing what he is signing, for such purchases as home intercoms or burglar alarm systems, which turn out to be defective or overpriced.

A common problem is that if the homeowner is not satisfied with the work or product or believes he has been cheated on price, any threats he makes to stop payment until he gets satisfaction are meaningless—because the merchant has sold the debt and mortgage to a finance company that is not legally responsible for anything the merchant may have done incorrectly. The finance company has the right to foreclose on the mortgage and auction off the house if the homeowner does not pay; the homeowner's only recourse is to sue the original merchant or home improvement firm, which, as often as not, is no longer in existence, its enriched operators having fled town after completing several similar transactions.

In many states, especially in the South and along the northern Atlantic seaboard, it is not even necessary for a finance company or collection agency to hold a mortgage before it can auction off a house for satisfaction of a debt. Hundreds of homeowners have had their houses sold out from under them, often without notice, at "sheriff's sales." Often the cause is a disputed bill for medical services or the like. If the homeowner does not pay, the creditor goes to the local court, produces proof of the unpaid debt, and obtains an order for the county sheriff to auction off the debtor's house. The auction is held in the sheriff's office and is usually lightly attended. Sometimes, a bidder can pick up a house for a few hundred dollars plus the existing mortgages on it and wipe out years and thousands of dollars of equity invested by the homeowner.

What can the victim do to fight these injustices? Hire a lawyer and go to court, of course. Trust that the lawyer will be honest with him. Wait in line at court. Hope that, in the end, the law protects him rather than his predator. Pay the lawyer's fee.

Even if everything else goes all right, that last step can undo it all. The lawyer's fee can cost more than is gained by the point won in court; it can cut disastrously into damages awarded a wronged client. Many middle-class citizens refuse to turn to the law for help when they need it because of the cost of a lawyer.

In most other countries of the world, the winner in a civil case can charge his attorney's fee and court costs to the loser. Why can't it be done that way in the United States? It would eliminate the need for the contingency fee. It also would encourage wronged citizens to go to court to seek redress when their chances of winning were obviously great, whereas now they hesitate because they must pay their lawyer out of what they win.

A person uncertain about his chances might still stay away from court, if he faced paying stiff legal fees in a losing cause. The answer to that might be to combine the principle that the winner's legal fees are paid by the loser with group legal aid for the middle class. Union or professional association members, for instance, could pay into a pool to hire lawyers on retainer to represent members in any private litigation, much as an employer's "house counsel" does for executives of a firm. When members won in court, the fees paid by the loser would go back into the pool. If a losing case particularly taxed the lawyer's time, the member-litigant could reimburse the pool as much as his individual income allowed. The system could be set up much like group insurance or an employees' credit union.

Large groups of middle-class people hiring lawyers on retainer could mean an end to bonanza fees in individual cases, and the beginning of price competition as these groups search for the best talent for their retainer dollar. As matters now stand, lawyers have rules that do not allow this cost-cutting practice. Most local bar associations forbid their members undercutting each other on price for "standard" kinds of cases such as probate and divorce. In fact, the lawyers of many states have adopted "minimum fee schedules" for these cases, and no lawyer is allowed to charge less. Frequently, the minimums are enforced by local judges in court. "The habitual charging of fees less than those established by a minimum fee schedule, or the charging of such fees without proper justification, may be evidence of unethical conduct," declared the American Bar Association's Committee on Professional Ethics and Grievances in 1961. (If the same thing were going on in another trade, the lawyers would doubtless call it price-fixing.)

At the gates of the American court system today, the beleaguered middle-class citizen is as much a "little man" as his poorer neighbors. He can only hope that the legal profession will eventually take to heart what an immigrant lawyer and noted reformer passionately deplores having been allowed to happen in this of all nations. To quote what Professor Albert A. Ehrensweig, of the University of California, Berkeley, once wrote for the *University of California Law Review:* "Strangely, terribly, intolerably, these United States, this citadel of democracy, which has taken it on itself to play the decisive role in building the Rule of Law throughout the world, has forgotten the little man in his struggle for civil justice."

VI

What Century Is the Courthouse in?

Former Chief Justice Earl Warren of the U.S. Supreme Court once told a group of judges and lawyers about a study made of a crowded trial court in a large East Coast city. The clerk's office was particularly chaotic and backward in its operation. Observers had noticed that one deputy clerk, whose desk was next to the wall, frequently left the room for short periods in response to a loud knocking from the other side of the wall. "In due course, the reason for the mysterious conduct was disclosed," Warren said. "On the other side of the wall was the probation office, which had a telephone, while there was no telephone in the clerk's office. Consequently, knowledgeable lawyers who needed to telephone to the clerk's office would call the probation officer who would knock on the wall so that the deputy clerk would come to answer the phone.

"This strange practice arose," Warren explained, "because the clerk did not permit a telephone in the office. He said he was opposed to the telephone on principle. This incident is not from the Dark Ages. It happened as recently as 1958."

Although most court offices do have telephones, to step inside the local courthouse, in this age of space travel, transoceanic television, and computers, is to travel backward in time—if not to the Dark Ages, then certainly to an era generations ago. Modern improvements in management techniques, record-keeping, and communications are all but unheard of inside courthouse walls. Instead, U.S. courts continue to follow slavishly many of the same procedures as did courts in early rural America and the shires of England before that.

Time and motion are wasted and serious errors risked at every stage of civil and criminal cases by outmoded methods and unnecessary formalities, paper work, and special privileges for judges, lawyers, and courthouse personnel. Cases are postponed repeatedly as delays grow from weeks and months into years. Participants and court documents frequently become lost in the system.

Words and decisions in the courtroom are set down by hand and transported through the courthouse on foot, as they have been for untold years. It takes hours for papers to be moved about and cases processed before court can open in the morning and close down at night, and months before transcripts can be typed up for appeals. Longhand notations of a judge's action become illegible, and records are misplaced, sometimes forever.

Thick case files are filled with unnecessary but still required pieces of paper and stored in file cabinets by case number. It can take half an hour to locate a piece of information for a single case in most courthouses. Collecting any one category of data from a large sample of cases—such as the lengths of sentences given robbery defendants over a year's time—requires weeks or months of random searching, if it can be done at all. Many courts are unable even to count accurately how many cases are begun and completed each year or to measure how long it takes an average case to reach trial.

Despite large increases in work loads, the pace of courts remains traditionally slow. Judges usually do not ascend to their benches before 10 A.M. or stay past 4 P.M. "You could shoot a cannon off in the courthouse at 4:30 and not hit anyone," observed a judge in Washington, D.C. Lunch hours and recesses are long, and judges take days off in the middle of the week when they want to. Summer often brings an almost complete halt to all but emergency business, as most judges take their vacations of a month or two at the same time. No one in the courthouse supervises judges' working hours or schedules their comings or goings. As one veteran clerk says, "No matter how late it is when a judge gets on the bench in the morning, that's when it's ten o'clock."

What management there is of the operation of most courts is performed by amateurs. The chief, or presiding judge—who often is selected from among the court's jurists simply on the basis of seniority—has never had any kind of management training. The courthouse clerks are usually equally untrained and frequently are political-party workers rewarded for their labors with appointment to a court job or nomination to an elected clerkship. Some court employees are swamped with work, while many, especially the traditional courtroom bailiffs, do nothing but stand idle all day.

The chief clerks in many courts are legally empowered to act independently of directives from the presiding judge, and they become powerful satraps who jealously guard their prerogatives and resist change. In many courts, if the presiding judge wishes to speed up the court's operation by changing record-keeping in a certain way—such as maintaining records by typewriter or data-processing rather than by hand—a clerk who dislikes the reform can refuse to cooperate. It took Chief Justice Warren three years to get a typewriter into the clerk's office at the U.S. Supreme Court and to stop the making of docket entries in longhand there.

Edward Gallas, the first management specialist to work as a court administrator in this country, helped reorganize the Los Angeles courts. He likes to tell of the time he was invited to Texas, where the state's governing body of judges wanted him to suggest ways to improve the administration of their chaotic court system. When Gallas urged that a certain new method of keeping records and statistics be tried, he was quickly told it would not work. "Why?" Gallas asked. "Because our clerks won't report it this way," the judges said.

"Well, fire them," Gallas suggested. "They're supposed to work for the courts, aren't they?"

But a judge answered, "Oh, no, we can't. They are elected clerks."

The lack of over-all direction and coordination in each courthouse means that cases are scheduled and heard almost by chance. First, they are put on a waiting list for a future hearing or trial date. On that day, the judge calls each case on the list in order. He may or may not reach them all. If he fails to finish the list, no one else calls the leftover cases. They are postponed and added to another waiting list for another day—when again any one case may not be reached.

More often than not, the majority of cases on the list are postponed, anyway, because a witness, civil litigant, or criminal defendant free on bail fails to show up—frequently because he was notified to come to court the wrong day or to the wrong courtroom—or because an attorney juggling several cases at once is tied up in another court or at his office. Other persons involved in the case who do show up are forced to come back another day.

Many attorneys knowingly take on too many cases and wind up with several scheduled simultaneously each day, so that all but one or two must be postponed. Often, lawyers make it into the courtroom only to ask for a delay because they have not yet finished preparing the case, they have not been paid their fee in advance, or they hope to gain some tactical advantage by waiting. Whatever the reason, or even if there really is no cause but negligence, one lawyer's request for a postponement is nearly always honored by the opposing lawyer. This is in keeping with traditional court-house courtesy; the accommodating lawyer will probably want the favor returned soon. A judge seldom takes it upon himself to overrule lawyers who agree on postponing a case —another courthouse tradition accepted almost everywhere —no matter what harm the delay may mean to the criminal defendant or civil litigant.

If, as is often the case, there are so many postponements that a judge moves quickly through his calendar for the day, no one brings him more cases. The judge sits idle or goes home early. Thus, in courthouses where files are overflowing with untried cases, a visitor can find courtroom after court-room empty by midday, despite the huge backlogs of cases that need a judge's urgent attention—simply because no more lawyers, witnesses, and litigants were notified to come to court that day. Although there are probably few court clerks who still ban telephones or typewriters from their offices, there seem to be many who refuse to use them to put lawyers, litigants, and witnesses on call for a certain day or group of days and then to take the trouble to summon them to the courthouse when necessary.

When a case is postponed again and again, witnesses who keep making fruitless trips to court often give up and do not return, thereby, in many criminal cases, forcing prosecutors to drop the charges against defendants because there are no longer witnesses to testify against them. Knowledgeable criminal defendants try to take advantage of the system's delays and frequently to create a few of their own. They outwait government witnesses or force a prosecutor who is worried that he will lose the case through default to agree to concessions in sentencing in return for a guilty plea. Some defendants encourage their lawyers to devise ways to keep postponing their cases until they come up before the most lenient judges—a common practice made possible by the confusion and delays. Less knowledgeable defendants, however, usually newcomers to the courthouse, wait unnecessarily for months in jail for trials delayed by the system itself or by their lawyers' unchecked negligence. Some eventually agree to decidedly unattractive bargains for guilty pleas just to end their ordeal.

Witnesses in civil cases often must be paid extra fees by litigants or their attorneys to continue to show up after repeated postponements. In New York, Philadelphia, Chicago, and other cities, citizens who go to court to recover for injuries suffered in accidents are forced to wait as long as five to ten years to take their claims before a judge. As the years go by, a large majority give up and agree to settle out of court, often for less than their actual losses.

"Interminable and unjustifiable delays in our courts," former Chief Justice Warren has said, "are today compromising the basic legal rights of countless thousands of Americans and, imperceptibly, corroding the very foundations of Constitutional government in the United States."

Imagine the bitterness of an innocent man jailed for a year or longer before he is given the opportunity to defend himself in court. Or the bravado of a young criminal who discovers that he can repeatedly violate the law with little or no retribution if he makes clever use of the chaos and delay in criminal court. Or the diminishing faith in the law experienced by the citizen who comes to court seeking redress of a wrong done him, only to be shunted aside for years before getting his claim in front of a judge and jury.

Society pays dearly for the continuing crimes of embittered and emboldened convicts returned to the streets, for the time wasted by policemen in court, for a growing middle-class impatience with the courts, and for the lost wages of good citizens who agree to serve as witnesses only to make repeated fruitless trips to court. The highest price of all, of course, is paid by the man accused of a crime who must wait months for trial. "Whether [he is] ultimately adjudged guilty or innocent, days drift by while his status remains unclarified," noted the report of the President's Commission on Law Enforcement and the Administration of Justice. "His job is lost. Bills and obligations accumulate. His family is unprovided for; it may start to disintegrate or become dependent on public assistance."

Justice slips away as time overtakes court cases that have not been acted on for years. A New York City court official said of the thousands of civil cases that have been pending there for more than five years, "At the end of that time, memories fade, witnesses forget the details, and the case becomes an envelope full of papers with numbers and dates on it."

"Delay breeds cynicism about justice," Columbia University law professor Maurice Rosenberg has written in one of his many studies of the problem (published in Jones, *The Courts, the Public, and the Population Explosion*). "We become used to the wrong and accept it."

We "become used to it" because "the law's delay," as Hamlet lamented, has been a burden for civilized man almost since courts were first established. Roman emperors, Goethe, Dickens, Kafka, and students of American justice beginning with Roscoe Pound in the early 1900's have complained of it. Successive Presidential commissions have found court delays among the underlying causes of crime, rioting, and widespread disrespect for the law in the United States in the 1960's.

But the fact that delay has always been with us is no reason why something can not be done about it now. The British, for instance, have progressed considerably from the time when the lethargy of Chancery Court was castigated by Dickens in his *Bleak House* account, only partially fictional, of the endless litigation of "Jarndyce vs. Jarndyce." Today, criminal cases in Britain are often completed, including disposition of an appeal, in as little as four months from the time of arrest—less than one fourth the average for criminal cases in American urban courts. At a time when man's accumulated knowledge and technological advancement are so great, why should widespread inefficiency and mismanagement be tolerated in U.S. courts?

It seems frighteningly obvious, in this increasingly critical time in the history of the United States, when the stresses of rising crime and social unrest are putting the courts to a crucial test, that the debilitating effects of delays could, as former Chief Justice Warren has warned, be disastrous to the nation. Yet delays in American courts continue to grow worse than ever before. Every year in Philadelphia, it takes a month longer than it did the previous year for the average civil case to reach a judge and jury for trial. Every month in Los Angeles, the backlog of untried civil and criminal cases grows by at least 200—and is now nearing a staggering 50,000 pending cases. In New York City, where about 10,000 defendants are waiting behind bars to be tried—2,000 of them for periods longer than six months—rioting in the city's jails in late 1970 dramatized the frustration.

Part of the cause for the steady and recently dramatic worsening of the delays in our courts is the startling increase in their business during the last several years due to continuing population growth, increasing urbanization and crime, and the growing numbers of suits being filed by poor people and others newly enabled to go to court more frequently when they need to. Recent appellate court rulings also have encouraged more criminal defendants and civil litigants to insist on trials by jury and to appeal decisions that go against them—rights guaranteed by the Constitution.

Some who wish to avoid taking the responsibility for the shocking delays and the drastic reforms that must be made to combat them attach too much importance to these factors, however. They refuse to admit that the primary cause of congestion and delay in American courts is what it has always been: the base inefficiency and unresponsiveness of the courts themselves, and the indifference of a citizenry that refuses both to attack the courts' lethargy and to pay for the increased personnel and modern machinery needed.

Cases pile up because the methods for moving them to trial are archaic, feeble, and slow. Cases are postponed when ready for trial because judges will not work full, properly scheduled days and lawyers, greedy for too many cases at one time, miss court appearances or come unprepared. Cases are lost in the system because judges and clerks with no management skills are trying to run a large, complicated business.

Tragically, the response to these problems in most American courts has not been to modernize an outmoded system but rather to short-circuit it. Pressures are being increased to end criminal cases short of trial with bargained guilty pleas and to complete civil suits quickly with compromise settlements. Appellate courts are becoming increasingly indulgent about these short cuts, and court officials keep trying to institutionalize them.

In Los Angeles, for instance, judges themselves sit in on criminal-case plea bargaining. In Detroit, the district attorney has a special office for this purpose. In Washington, D.C., the U.S. attorney has established formalized plea-bargaining procedures for his prosecutors and defense attorneys.

Everywhere, judges are pushing for faster settlement of more civil cases before trial with a device that is now forty years old but is being used more widely today than ever— the pretrial conference. At an informal meeting, often held in the judge's chambers, both sides present a summary of their cases, without observing strict legal procedures, and the judge tries to hammer out a settlement. One side offers a certain dollar amount, the other side counteroffers, and the judge suggests compromises. It is not unusual for a judge to twist a litigant's arm by warning him that he is unlikely to win any more money at a trial, which the same judge would conduct, than if he settles now. Pretrial conferences were first begun in the 1930's, to allow the two sides to discard unnecessary issues, agree on certain obvious facts, and provide the judge with helpful background on the case. But today they have become what one judge has called "fish market" proceedings.

It may be that, in many cases, justice would be better served if methods such as plea bargaining in criminal cases or pretrial arbitration of civil suits were refined, fitted out with rules of procedure acceptable under the Constitution, and substituted for trials. It can be argued that the present combat theory of adversary justice—as carried out in practice with the theatrics and obfuscations of lawyers determined to win at all costs in front of confused and belabored jurors—is not the best way to find truth or assure justice. But the replacement of judicial processes rooted in the Constitution should be made only after they have been carefully studied and steps have been taken to protect the rights of each defendant and litigant. Quick short cuts are not the way to cope with court congestion.

Pleas and out-of-court settlements have already replaced trials in nine of every ten court cases. Rules of due process are seldom followed, what is said and done in the bargaining process is seldom recorded for later review, and settled cases usually cannot be appealed. Little systematic study has been made of these short cuts or their consequences; no amendments have been made in court rules or the federal or state constitutions to establish them as accepted means of conducting court business in place of trials by jury. Instead, these measures have been taken in desperate haste and have grown like wild mushrooms in the fertile darkness of overcrowded courts.

One jurist who has been caught up in the battle against court delays, Bernard Botein, the former presiding judge of trial courts in Manhattan, is now alarmed by the short cuts he and other judges have taken. "Like most big-city administrators, I have utilized every device and contrivance I could copy to speed the disposition of cases and have even invented a gimmick or two myself," Botein told the New York City bar in 1966, "and now I fear that in doing so we have done the courts a great disservice." He continued:

> Too many judges have been caught up in a consuming campaign against That Old Debbil Calendar. . . . The frenzy with which we try to shorten the long line of cases shuffling toward trial, when it is accomplished by hard-pressed settlements, is highly indecorous and undignified. . . . Instant justice, at trial or pretrial stage, can never be a consistent substitute for a true justice, which requires time for brewing, blending, and often brooding.

Reducing some delay and trying to keep up with the influx of new cases in New York, Botein told the city's lawyers, was accomplished at the cost of "converting our courthouses into counting houses."

Professor Rosenberg concluded that "among the costs of the obsession with speedier justice has been an erosion of the judicial process from the viewpoint of the litigants and lawyers, some of whom have the impression that the courts regard their cases as merely counters in a numbers game."

The pathetic but instructive irony is that, even as more short cuts are tried and more pressure is applied, the delays grow still longer. Besides constituting dangerous tinkering with the fundamental processes of the court system, the short cuts amount to no more than halfway measures that threaten to erode further the quality of justice without really solving problems of quality. Crash campaigns begun by Botein, for instance, cut delays in New York City's trial courts briefly in the mid-1960's, but they now are growing again. And studies show that wherever pretrial conferences to pressure civil case settlements have been tried, delays for these cases on the whole were not significantly reduced.

Advocates of such short cuts as compromise settlements in civil cases and guilty pleas to criminal charges have created, in the legal and the public mind, a false notion of conflict between court efficiency and guaranteed due process. They argue that it is not possible to give everyone a trial or follow appellate court guidelines for protecting the rights of an accused criminal or wronged consumer and at the same time expect court proceedings to be speedily conducted. They are shutting their eyes to reforming courthouse management, hiring more judges and other personnel, and introducing modern equipment as ways to expedite court business.

Similarly, other voices in the legal community are urging changes that can be considered to be much more progressive than plea bargaining or forced settlements with the argument that they will reduce court congestion and delay. One of these suggested reforms is the replacement of fault-based automobile insurance with insurance that pays each driver and passenger for his loss no matter who is at fault, which would do away with litigation over who caused each accident and remove hundreds of thousands of civil cases from the courts. Another is the removal of the criminal sanction from alcoholism, narcotics addiction, gambling, and certain sex acts; legalizing these "crimes" and treating those of them that are truly social problems with other than legal remedies would reduce by the hundreds of thousands the criminal cases that now enter the courts each year. At the same time, these reforms would undoubtedly produce justice more often for affected citizens than the courts now manage—the real reason that they should be considered, more important by far than the possible dramatic reduction in the work load of the courts, significant as that would be.

All such proposals "deserve attention in their own right

and on the merits, and not because of some adventitious connection with the delay issue," Rosenberg has pointed out. "We should not redesign the basic architecture of our legal system simply to solve the homely problem of delay."

The obvious, if homely, solution is to yank the courts, and those who run them, into the twentieth century. And the task of modernization must begin with a reorganization of the basic U.S. court system.

The continuing imposition of a structure from the rural past has produced fragmented and overlapping jurisdictions among the courts of the cities, suburbs, counties, states, and the federal system. Often, there is doubt as to where a criminal should be tried or a civil case filed. Sometimes, a case already under way in one court must be moved to another and begun anew.

In nearly every city and in most small towns and rural areas, there are "inferior" courts that try the lowest levels of cases—suits for small amounts and petty crimes. In a city, this task may be carried out by a police court for criminal cases and a civil court for small-claims cases and landlord and tenant suits, each with full-time judges. In suburbs, small towns, and rural hamlets, the "lowest" court may be only a justice of the peace, who often is not a lawyer. Some follow legal procedures fairly closely, others not at all. A very few big-city inferior courts make written records of the cases before them and have a full complement of such supporting court personnel as clerks, probation officers, and the like, but most do not. Justices of the peace hardly ever do. Often, the border between a city and a suburb separates one form of lower court justice from a vastly different kind.

In addition, in each county of many states, there is an intermediate court that handles slightly more serious criminal cases and damage suits for higher amounts. In many counties, its geographical jurisdiction may overlap areas served by dozens of inferior courts, and not infrequently its legal jurisdiction also includes the same petty cases the inferior courts hear. This means that some cases can be taken into either court, depending on where an arresting officer or litigant chooses to go. Most county courts have full-time lawyers serving as judges, although a few do not. The quality and quantity of other personnel and the extent to which strict legal procedures are followed differs considerably from county to county, even within the same state. The differences are much wider between the county courts and the inferior courts that share jurisdictions with them.

Finally, each state also has a statewide court system, with an appellate court (usually called the state supreme court) at the top of the pyramid and several trial courts at the bottom. Each trial court (usually called a circuit or superior court) has general jurisdiction over all kinds of law cases within the boundaries it serves—which can be a county, a group of counties, or an arbitrarily marked off section of the state that does not follow county lines. Serious criminal cases and civil suits for large dollar amounts usually can be tried only in these courts. In many states, these courts can also exercise jurisdiction over petty cases, along with both county and inferior courts, giving litigants and police a third place to go with these cases.

Even within a single court in some cities, a case must also be moved through several branches of that court before it is tried. In New York City, for instance, a criminal case must go through at least four: In one branch, the defendant is first brought before a judge to state his plea; in another, he is given a preliminary hearing; in another, the trial date is set (unless the defendant pleads guilty at this stage, as many are encouraged to do); and, in still another, the trial actually takes place. More often than not, at least one postponement occurs at each stage. Defendants, lawyers, witnesses, and policemen must usually return to court six to ten times before each case is completed.

There is no over-all management control of the various

kinds of courts that exist within each state. There is no uniform standard for the qualifications of judges, the transcribing of courtroom testimony, the supplying of a lawyer to criminal defendants who cannot afford one, the legal procedures to be followed, or any other court function. The quality of justice a criminal defendant or civil litigant receives depends on which court he lands in—which, in turn, is determined by the seriousness of the crime, the amount of the civil suit, the whim or wisdom of a policeman or lawyer, or the accident of geography.

What is needed is for each state to reorganize its courts in line with a model system, such as the one proposed by the American Bar Association. A few states, led by California and Illinois, have at least partially reorganized their courts. To work best, a state system should provide the same kind of superior court for every county or judicial district in the state, with identical branches wherever needed for smaller geographical areas on the basis of population. Branches that try only petty cases, especially those involving the poor, should be located close to where people live in their neighborhoods, and each case should begin and end in a single branch. Every court and branch should have similarly qualified judges, provide a full range of court services with professional personnel, and follow to the letter uniform rules of legal procedure. The entire system should be under the central administrative control of a state management office that would oversee professional administrators in each local court, keep statistics, make court studies, and direct management changes from the state level. State systems should match, so that the quality of justice does not change when a state border is crossed.

Everything that every court does, except for the case-by-case decision-making by a judge, should be under the direction of professional court administrators trained in both management techniques and some law. Each court's administrator should be empowered to hire, fire, and direct the work of all clerks, each of whom should also have appropriate training in data-processing or whatever speciality is needed. These jobs could provide a useful and attractive outlet for trade school graduates. The administrators should also schedule the working hours of judges. They should be responsible to the presiding judge of the court and to state court officials for ensuring that every case receives a hearing and trial by certain deadlines, with extensions granted only by a judge, whose decision could then be appealed by either party in the case to a higher court. The deadlines (for the intervals between case filing to first hearing, to trial, and finally to appeal) should be set on a state-wide basis. Each court administrator should report regularly and publicly on whether the deadlines are being met and what is needed (more judges, for instance) to catch up when they are being missed.

Lawyers must agree, or be compelled to do so by law or court rule, to take on and schedule cases within quotas set by the trial courts in which they appear. They must show up and be prepared for every scheduled court appearance, under strict penalties for contempt of court whenever they fail to do so. When they declare that they are ready for trial, they must come to court on the day the trial is to begin ready to try the case. Bluffing readiness for trial, a common ploy that today compounds congestion and delay, should be treated by the law and judges as perjury and punished accordingly. To make all this possible and to prevent lawyers from scheduling several cases or court hearings simultaneously, each lawyer's case load and court dates should be regulated by court administrators.

Such strict and sophisticated management would be possible if computerized data-processing, a necessity today for any large business or governmental agency, were introduced into the courts. At the very least, all court records should be duplicated in computer information banks, making it possible to determine how many cases each attorney has and when each case is scheduled for its next court hearing. Each attorney's case load could be printed out regularly. One copy could be used by a court administrator, who would check for violations of case load or scheduling rules; another could be sent to the lawyer to remind him of his court schedule. A computer system could also address the envelopes.

Similarly, computers could be used to print out a daily calendar for each judge, to provide additional information on case loads so that the judge's time could be properly scheduled, and to produce lists of backup cases, complete with the telephone numbers of the principals and lawyers involved so that they could be called to court by phone if all other cases scheduled for that day were completed before closing time.

If certain important facts about each case in court were fed into a computer data bank, it would take only seconds to find out, for instance, whether court deadlines are being met, how many damage suits arise from swimming-pool accidents in a year and how they are resolved, how many defendants were arrested for carrying guns during a certain period and what happened to them in court, the average sentence meted out for a certain crime by different judges. The computer would enable a court for the first time to know exactly what it does each day and how it does it— much as insurance companies can use computerized data banks to check quickly on what policies they have in force, what kinds of people hold them, what their payment records are, and how often, for what kind of occurrences, and in what amounts claims are paid. Administrators could then determine accurately how well each court is coping with its business, whether methods need to be changed, or whether more judges are needed.

It might even be possible for the cumbersome and wasteful handling of court paper records to be reduced or eliminated by computers. If the vital information for each case were stored in a computer bank, it would be possible for a clerk in each courtroom to punch up the needed data instantly on a console screen as each case is called or to have it printed out in paper form. Action taken on the case that day could then be fed immediately into the computer bank by the same courtroom clerk. There would be no opportunity for the writing of illegible notes or the losing of papers on their way to the file room.

Courtroom stenography could be replaced or supplemented by sound recording and television taping. Tapes of requested portions could be shown to juries during their deliberations. Television tapes could be especially valuable in appeals of trial court cases. Not merely the words spoken, but also the telling gestures of participants and the emotional atmosphere of the trial, which are increasingly becoming issues on appeal, could be put before the appellate judges for review. The present delays of several months for each appeal while a transcript is being typed could be eliminated.

Legal procedures, too, could and should be modernized without distorting their substance. Much of the pleading that must be prepared and filed by lawyers today, greatly increasing delays and the paper load of the system, could be eliminated. As it now stands, these pleas unnecessarily duplicate courtroom argument, rephrase the language of past appellate rulings that could readily be found by judges and opposing attorneys in their lawbooks from brief citations provided in the pleadings, or reproduce word for word from law manuals standard legal formalities that have no bearing on the facts of a case.

Lawyers could be required to bring up and argue all the various motions they wish to make in a criminal or civil case (to challenge jurisdiction, discover parts of the other side's case, exclude certain evidence, challenge a criminal confession, and so on) in a single omnibus hearing at a set time before trial. At present, lawyers often drag out the filing and arguing of motions one at a time to create delay beneficial to their client or, sometimes, surprise the other side and lengthen trials by bringing up still more motions at the beginning of a trial. Some critics blame appellate courts for rulings that make more motions and, consequently, more delay possible. But it is the way lawyers are allowed to use a client's right to make these motions as a device for stalling or outwitting their opponents that causes the problems, and this practice can be stopped.

Every one of these ideas has been suggested, often in much more workable detail than outlined here, by lawyers, judges, and expert students of the courts, who support their arguments with the requisite legal rationale. The American Bar Association, for instance, has tried for decades to convince each state to adopt a model, unified structure for its courts. Chief Justice Earl Warren and Chief Justice Warren Burger have both championed the use of modern management techniques and computerized data-processing under the direction of professional administrators in the courts.

But very little progress has been made. The few scattered attempts at court reorganization across the country have been hampered by a proliferation of unnecessary branches within the new courts, as in Chicago and New York City, or continuing fragmented local control over court budgets and the election and legal independence of untrained court clerks, as in California. Computers have been introduced into only a handful of urban courts and, in most instances (Los Angeles, Chicago, and Washington, D.C., are examples), have been used thus far only to speed up old-fashioned clerical functions; the computer in Los Angeles, for instance, stores case information that must first be received by mail from court branches and is then still recorded by hand in docket books in duplication of the computer's work. Seldom are the computers that have been installed used to do anything new, such as overseeing attorneys' case loads, managing judges' time, devising efficient court calendars, replacing the storing of huge files of paper for each case, or making possible the fast retrieval of information about broad classes of cases.

Why is there so little change? One reason is money: Taxpayers seem uninterested in court problems (except for controversial Supreme Court decisions) and unenthusiastic about paying for computers, more judges, and trained personnel for reorganized courts. Many courts are already forced to run on the money they collect in fines. The police appear to have more sex appeal and are taking most of what extra money is now being spent on the administration of justice. The New York courts, for instance, received only $20,000 of the first $260,000 spent by the Mayor's Committee on Law Enforcement; courts across the country have received similarly small shares (about 10 per cent) of the money for new technology being distributed by the Justice Department's new Law Enforcement Assistance Administration.

Another important reason for the inertia is a singular lack of enthusiasm for reform among the rank and file of the legal establishment. Chief Justice Burger may call for change, but local lawyers and judges, who are close to and influential in the workings of local and state government, are not following his lead. Some of them, in the manner of the clerk who disliked telephones, resist having their sleepy courthouses invaded by modern technology. More do not want to lose long-enjoyed prerogatives. The computer in Los Angeles, for instance, cannot be used to print out standard forms for criminal case files because the city's criminal-court judges cannot agree on what the form should look like; each now uses a variation of his own. Judges do not want to be told by some efficiency expert when to come to work and how many cases to try. Lawyers in California struck down through the state bar association a rule requiring that lawyers be ready for trial when they promise to be or face indictment for perjury.

The ironies are tragic. Police are given more money and equipment to catch criminals faster, only to send them to courts that have not been similarly enabled to move swiftly. Judges and lawyers maintain complete freedom to come and go in court as they please, while citizens are high-pressured into giving up their right to trial by jury because the system is not running efficiently. Modern technology inundates courts with new litigation but cannot penetrate the courthouse walls.

The consequences are plain. If taxpayers and legal bureaucrats alike do not soon begin to make some sacrifices, so that the courts can be modernized, the nation may face an ugly dilemma. We can watch an increasingly overloaded judiciary system grind to a standstill. Or we can stand by while it is kept going only through panicky reliance on short-cut methods of adjudication that deny citizens their right to trial and mock justice in its own chambers.

VII

The Legal Bureaucrats

The chaotic trial courts of the United States—where ordinary citizens most often come into contact with the law—are the stagnant backwater of the country's legal profession. Very seldom do Americans brought to them by criminal prosecutions, accident injury suits, traffic citations, divorce cases, and other litigation find the wise, firm, carefully spoken judge, the determined and experienced district attorney, the shrewd and courageous defender of accused men after the pattern of Clarence Darrow, the diligent and trustworthy independent civil lawyer. Particularly in the large cities, the chances of encountering anybody resembling the mythical legal heroes of school books, fiction, television dramas, and Law Day orations are slim indeed.

Many trial court judges, elevated to the bench primarily because of their political ties or bar association popularity, are obviously lacking in judicial training and temperament. They have difficulty ruling correctly on routine legal questions. They fail to follow proper procedures, rush cases through without trials, arrogantly browbeat citizens and attorneys, and generally act more often out of expedience and prejudice than a sure sense of justice. Young, inexperienced prosecutors fail to ask key questions of witnesses or to make necessary objections during hearings and trials unless prompted by the more knowledgeable judges. Public defenders and independent, often avaricious criminal lawyers bargain away the right to trial for defendants whose names they frequently forget when standing before the judge to plead their hapless clients guilty. Self-employed civil lawyers—the descendants of the trusted town barrister whose shingle was hung proudly outside his busy law office—all too often overcharge, cheat, or negligently serve citizens forced to turn to them with their legal problems.

In the hands of legal bureaucrats of the trial courts, justice is subordinated to self-interest and bureaucratic ends, weakened by long delays and neglect, and finally trampled in the haste with which each day's assortment of stale cases is run through the mill.

Most of the nation's lawyers have little to do with the dispensing of trial court justice. They work in commerce and government, far removed from the hurly-burly of the trial courts and the legal cares of ordinary citizens. To these members of a lucrative profession, the law is a generally smooth-working system of negotiations and contracts. Their contact with the rest of the legal world is limited for the most part to law journals, appellate court decisions, and bar association gatherings. These attorneys are the Law Day orators who assure us that our legal processes ultimately produce justice for all. Common trials are events they read about in newspapers, and the local trial courts are vaguely known places that, in the words of one big-city bar association president, "I understand" are "sometimes like a jungle."

The corporation and government lawyers, as well as the bar associations and the law schools, have been content to leave the operation of the trial courts and the legal work of the vast majority of Americans to badly trained newcomers, inept has-beens, political lackeys, and sharp dealers. Some able practitioners and even a few idealistic reformers do appear in the trial courts. But usually they are swallowed up in the closed courthouse bureaucracy, which is composed not only of judges, prosecutors, public defenders, and their supporting personnel, but also the private-practice lawyers who appear regularly in the trial courts in divorce, accident injury, probate, and other cases.

This bureaucracy, like any other, is primarily self-serving and antagonistic to outside criticism or interference. It works more toward preserving itself and its habitual ways than serving the needs of the public or the ends of justice. Each member is primarily concerned with protecting his job and the special privileges he has always enjoyed despite his lack of training and the low level of competence he frequently demonstrates. Each is careful not to spoil things for the other.

When a judge is under pressure to process more cases faster, lawyers cooperate by agreeing to forgo trials; they press for hastily bargained guilty pleas in criminal cases and compromise settlements of civil suits. When a lawyer wants to delay because he is unprepared, trying to outwait the other side, or merely seeking time to extract a larger fee from a client, the judge and even the opposing lawyer often go along with him. When a judge or prosecutor persists in making serious courtroom errors, everyone else ignores these lapses and continues to pay each man the courtesy of his office. When a lawyer must be warned or reprimanded for especially grievous misconduct, the bar does its best to keep the proceedings a secret from the public.

Occasionally, someone in the system breaks form and threatens the *status quo,* only to find that he can accomplish little and will probably draw sharp reprisals from the rest of the bureaucracy. A criminal-court judge in Detroit, for instance, decided one day to stop sitting back mutely—as case after case ended with the defendant pleading guilty in exchange for the prosecutor's promise of leniency—and scolded the defense lawyers and prosecutors for failing to try cases in which, in the judge's opinion, the defendant

might well be acquitted. Next day, the court's presiding
judge replaced the dissenting judge on the bench and made
a show of approving all bargained pleas as fast as they were
brought before him. In New York City, a few Legal Aid lawyers threatened to strike if someone did not do something
about rushing cases through hearings in criminal court so
fast that the lawyers could not give each case sufficient attention. They were ignored. New York arraignment courtrooms, where Legal Aid lawyers work ten hours a day with
defendants, still process nearly 300 cases per courtroom per
day—an average of one every two minutes. In Washington,
D.C., a few judges on the local trial court began reprimand-
ing those lawyers who failed to show up for scheduled court
hearings and trials or who were obviously handling a client's
case badly in court. After a few months of this effort, the
local trial bar announced that it would investigate the conduct of the court's judges and possibly recommend that
some be removed.

"The only sensible thing was to adapt oneself to existing
conditions," Kafka wrote more than fifty years ago in *The
Trial*. He could have been describing American trial courts
today:

> Even if it were possible to alter a detail for the better here or
> there—but it was simply madness to think of it—any benefit
> arising from that would profit clients in the future only, while
> one's own interests would be immeasurably injured by attract-
> ing the attention of the ever-vengeful officials. Anything
> rather than that! One must lie low, no matter how much it
> went against the grain, and try to understand that this great
> organization remained, so to speak, in a state of delicate bal-
> ance, and that if someone took it upon himself to alter the
> disposition of things around him, he ran the risk of losing his
> footing and falling to destruction, while the organization would
> simply right itself by some compensating reaction in another
> part of the machinery—since everything interlocked—and re-
> main unchanged, unless, indeed, which was very probable, it

became still more rigid, more vigilant, severer, and more ruthless.

In the end, sociologist Abraham Blumberg declares, "the client becomes a secondary figure in the court system," along with the public interest and the ideal of justice. In his study of the American criminal-court process, *Criminal Justice,* Blumberg concludes that

> the client may present doubts, contingencies, and pressures which challenge or disrupt. But they are usually resolved in favor of the organization. Even the [client's] lawyer has far greater professional, economic and other ties to the various elements of the court system than to his own client. In short, the court is a closed community.

The system remains closed essentially because of the inaction of the legal profession. One reason, of course, is that many lawyers simply want to avoid contact with the judiciary "jungle." Just as important is the fact that significantly reforming the operation of our trial courts and improving the conduct of the lawyers and judges who work in them would necessitate drastic changes in the present training, structure, and discipline of the American bar. With the possible exception of Ralph Nader, even the most radical of the new breed of public-service-minded young lawyers have thus far shown no willingness to attempt or even to suggest any such cataclysmic internal professional upheaval.

The roots of the problem reach all the way down into the nation's law schools, which simply do not prepare their graduates for service in or toward the improvement of the trial courts.

The average law school curriculum offers a plethora of courses in commercial, contract, property, accident injury, tax, estate, government, constitutional, and international law. Some of the bigger law schools today have also begun to teach poverty law. The overwhelming emphasis throughout is on how appellate courts decided certain kinds of legal disputes in the past—and why. Each student must memorize these cases and learn how to fit any hypothetical or real case into one of the molds. He (or, increasingly, she) is taught that thinking like a lawyer means seeing each controversy as an adversary situation with two legally arguable sides supported by past court decisions—rather than as a problem of social importance with some single preferable solution. The existing legal system is accepted as a given, with unchangeable parameters to which the aspiring lawyer must always conform. In the law school classroom, all thought contexts and questions are supplied by the instructor, who subtly channels the student's thinking along the path of legal precedent. "Wasteful" excursions of initiative off the routes delineated by past cases is determinedly discouraged—when necessary by professional scolding and class embarrassment.

The law school microcosms seldom describe what actually happens in trial courts. The bulk of their cases are not the stuff of commercial law. Instead, they are criminal prosecutions, traffic violations, divorces, and the most legally simplistic accident-injury cases that involve merely the question of whose story is to be believed.

More than 90 per cent of all trial court cases—criminal and civil—are ended not by a courtroom trial or appellate court decision but by the default of one party or the other or by a negotiated compromise settlement. The outcome is shaped not so much by past court decisions on similar cases as by the pressures of heavy case loads, the sentencing bargain offered a criminal defendant, or a civil litigant's financial inability to wait out long delays. Even cases that do come to trial or are decided by a trial judge's ruling often end up a far cry from the law school casebook examples. Juries frequently depart from precedents set by judges in the past—as do the judges themselves, often because they are unfamiliar with, or care little about, legal precedents. Only a small fraction of these cases are ever appealed to provide an eventual opportunity for their final outcome to conform with law school precepts.

Law school prepares specialists for real estate law or income tax law; it gives little if any training for trial court practice as it is today. For instance, most law students get only a single cursory course in criminal law. Few graduates realize until they must stand beside a criminal defendant in court that most defendants plead guilty and that what the lawyer really must know is how to negotiate the most favorable sentence in exchange for a guilty plea. Not until lawyers first handle an automobile injury case do they discover that expert knowledge of the laws and case history on torts (in this case, accident liability) means less to the success of a client's claim than the attorney's negotiation techniques, his knowledge of medicine, his understanding of the technicalities of what happens when cars crash, and his courtroom showmanship. Today's law school graduates get their courtroom training from those law firms that provide it for new employees or from kindly elders at the courthouse. For many young trial lawyers, the process is essentially one of trial and error—and their first clients must bear the consequences of the errors.

The law schools also fail to provide special training for future judges, either for law students generally or for practicing lawyers who aspire, or are chosen, to be judges. The lower trial courts themselves are never studied as the legal and social phenomena that they are, so that law school graduates could know how to try cases properly in them or could work for reform of their grave deficiencies. The average law student is shielded from knowledge of the confusion, heavy case loads, long delays, incompetence, and compromises or outright denials of justice in American trial courts.

Why? Probably the simple reason is that few law school graduates become criminal lawyers. Therefore, the law schools provide little training in criminal law. The same is true for most civil proceedings in the trial courts, even though these courts touch many more lives in more meaningful ways and do more to determine the quality of justice in this nation dedicated to the Rule of Law than the sum total of all the contracts negotiated by commercial and government lawyers.

The "lack of attention to criminal, as compared to the emphasis on commercial, law," the President's Commission on Law Enforcement and the Administration of Justice noted, "may be partly explained by the bar's general disregard for the field and the lack of financial reward. Law schools feel obligated to provide training related to the work their graduates will do."

About 15 per cent of the nation's lawyers, according to most estimates, work for the government, the majority in jobs having little to do with the trial courts or the legal problems of the average citizen. More than three fourths of the other 85 per cent who are in private practice primarily work for business interests, in real estate, or handling the estates and trusts of the wealthy. Thus, there remains only one lawyer in five to work in the trial courts and with the legal business of ordinary Americans.

An exhaustive survey of the New York City bar by lawyer-sociologist Jerome E. Carlin in the mid-1960's (published in his *Lawyer's Ethics*) showed that 45 per cent of the private-practice lawyers there specialize in commercial law, another 14 per cent in real estate and 17 per cent in probate and trusts. These attorneys, Carlin found, include nearly all of those who work in the bigger firms, earn the higher salaries and fees, are graduates of the better law schools, and are considered by their peers to be the more able practitioners of the law. They are, Carlin noted, the "elite segment of the bar."

The remaining one-fourth of New York City's private bar, according to Carlin's survey, are primarily occupied with accident injury, divorce, criminal, and other trial court litigation. These lawyers work primarily alone or in small firms, the study showed, earn lower incomes among attorneys, and are considered by other lawyers to be less competent, less well trained, and on lower rungs of the professional ladder. Thus it is a small and distinctly less able fraction of the New York City bar that undertakes the legal work for the majority of the users of the city's trial courts.

In addition, Carlin's study showed, these are the lawyers who are most likely to breach the bar's written rules of legal ethics and fail to serve their clients faithfully. Geoffrey C. Hazard, Jr., executive director of the American Bar Foundation, noted, in his introduction to Carlin's book, "The lawyer most prone to ethical deviation is the lawyer who is on his own or in a small firm, representing 'ordinary' clients in the ordinary courts and agencies concerning . . . ordinary matters such as personal injury claims. . . ." On the basis of more limited studies and observations elsewhere, Hazard also concluded that Carlin's findings could be applied to this segment of the bar nationally. "It is surely a disconcerting revelation," he wrote, "that the lawyer whose situation in practice most nearly approximates the traditional ideal of what it should be is also the lawyer most susceptible to violation of the traditional ideal of what his conduct should be."

The large "elite" segment of the bar, however, as Carlin himself noted, "is able to insulate itself from ethically contaminating influences," such as uncertainty of income, which can lead to high-pressure fee-collecting, overcharging, or tampering with clients' funds, and the pressures from other members of the legal bureaucracy in the crowded trial courts to compromise client or public interest to cope with case backlogs, long delays, and the generally low level of legal competence. "Lower-status lawyers are forced to bear the brunt of these pressures," Carlin pointed out. "In the process they become deprofessionalized."

Carlin's unsettling if not unexpected conclusion is that

> The best trained, most technically skilled, and ethically most responsible lawyers are reserved [for] the upper reaches of business and society. This leaves the least competent, least well-trained, and least ethical lawyers to the lower-income individuals.

They are also left to the trial courts, where they inevitably become part of the courthouse legal bureaucracy. Their clients come and go, but the other lawyers, judges, and court personnel these lawyers deal with remain the same. Every day, they conspire together in the compromises that keep the system going for them. They help cover up each other's mistakes and misconduct. And they are permitted to go on this way by the profession's larger elite, because it is not anxious to come to grips with the great underlying problems of the trial courts and is therefore willing to overlook and even help keep from public view misconduct among lawyers in the courtrooms.

The results of Carlin's study, as well as others, show that there is much discrepancy between the ethical standards that lawyers profess to follow and their actual conduct. Carlin estimates violations by 22 per cent of the private New York City bar, pointing out that even this figure may be an underestimation because it is based on what the lawyers themselves anonymously admitted to in his survey. Thus, at least 20,000 lawyers in Manhattan and the Bronx alone, where Carlin's study was conducted, consciously misrepresent their clients, misuse entrusted funds, try to corrupt officials and other lawyers, solicit clients improperly, or otherwise break the legal profession's own rules of professional conduct.

Few lawyers report misconduct by other lawyers except when improper solicitation of clients is involved, and many clients themselves either condone violations of ethics—those they believe help their cases—or fail to discover those that harm them. Nevertheless, bar associations and grievance committees across the country, few of which take pains to make their existence and whereabouts known to the public, receive thousands of client complaints about their lawyers' conduct.

Clients complain about the size of the fees they have been charged or about not being informed for months or years of the progress of their cases. Sometimes, they discover that their cases have been lost in court because their lawyers failed to file necessary papers on time or were otherwise negligent. Some lawyers are caught stealing from estates to be probated or misusing funds intended for settlement of an accident injury claim, the purchase of a house, or the premium on a bail bond. Occasionally, a case achieves notoriety and surfaces in the newspapers or courts: three lawyers arrested in Maryland for misusing money entrusted to them for home purchases; several indicted in New York for stealing the inheritance of their clients; a Washington, D.C., lawyer exposed for pressuring exorbitant fees from traffic offenders who feared losing their licenses in court. Once made public, such deeds usually bring punishment.

But few misbehaving lawyers are strongly dealt with. In New York City, according to figures from the bar discipline group there, only about 1 per cent of the lawyers against whom formal complaints are filed are ever censured, suspended, or disbarred. This also is about the average reported by those other jurisdictions in which the local bar will make relevant figures public. Many bar groups will not release any statistics. Many more will not reveal the names of lawyers disciplined unless and until the lawyers are finally disbarred. In addition, disciplinary action and public disclosure are usually suffered only by those lawyers who are discovered actually to have broken the law in their wrongdoing. Widespread unethical but legal cheating of clients and persistent negligence in the handling of cases are usually answered with, at most, private warnings from bar discipline groups.

In a few states, the bar has created, through contributions from lawyers, a fund to compensate clients who have suffered financial losses from the misconduct of their lawyers—including clients who have had inheritances stolen. Most of the funds contain too little money, however, to pay very many victims, and there is usually a flat limit on how much can be paid out in any single case—an amount that often is only a fraction of the loss actually suffered. Officials controlling these funds also refuse to make public any information about who applies to them for compensation or why. There is no way to know how many requests are turned away, who the wrongdoers are, or what they have done. A few funds merely announce that a particular claimant has been paid a certain amount, with no further explanation.

Many lawyers buy malpractice insurance, which does provide full compensation for the victim of an attorney's negligence—as for instance, when a prominent midwestern law firm lost a tax case file and was unable to collect a $100,000 tax refund for a client corporation. But, once again, the lawyers buying this insurance are usually the elite practitioners who can afford the premiums and who want to offer their clients such protection. The trial court lawyer often has neither insurance nor enough money of his own to compensate a wronged client. To make matters worse, in recent years, a large increase in claims being paid out for the mistakes of the big law firms has so taxed the few malpractice insurers that they have told lawyers that premium rates are likely to continue rising by 20 per cent to 100 per cent every year.

If the legal bureaucrats of the trial courts are driven out of law practice by closely enforced ethical and insuring requirements, who will be left to take over the relatively unremunerative, decidedly unglamorous work load in the "jungle"? The elite lawyers do not want to shoulder the responsibility. It is not quite "that the good lawyers all consciously delegate their dirty work to others (although many do)," sociologist Everett C. Hughes has written in *Men and Their Work*. "It is rather a game of live and let live. . . ."

No group of lawyers is left with as much dirty work as the small coterie that represents unmonied accused criminals in the trial courts. Most lawyers, poorly prepared in law school for criminal work in the first place, are averse to laboring in this field. Those who do so regularly are usually relegated to the bottom of the profession's pecking order. There are a few exceptions. Such criminal lawyers who are, in fact, part of the bar elite themselves, as Edward Bennett Williams, F. Lee Bailey, and Percy Foreman, usually represent defendants who can afford large fees. The cases they pick are often celebrated ones. Sometimes equally well paid, though obviously not so well thought of, are the lawyers who serve as "house counsel" for such professional criminals as narcotics dealers, gamblers, prostitutes, and even big-time holdup men. But these two disparate groups of criminal lawyers combined make up a tiny fraction of the bar, representing a small portion of the defendants brought to the trial courts each day. The vast majority of criminal defendants come to court without lawyers of their own. Because the Supreme Court has ruled that anyone being tried for a felony must be represented by a lawyer and many trial courts also expect persons charged with serious misdemeanors to have lawyers, a public defender or a private-practice lawyer is frequently appointed. A few self-employed criminal lawyers who work regularly in the criminal courts also find clients in the courthouse. Altogether, lawyers are provided in these two ways for an estimated 150,000 felony defendants and countless thousands of misdemeanor suspects in trial courts across the country.

A minority of defendants can afford to pay their lawyers something. From them, the private-practice attorneys who hang around the courthouse collect what they can. But an overwhelming majority of defendants have no money. They are represented by salaried public defenders or by private practice lawyers who may be paid fixed fees by the county, state, or federal government, or, in thousands of cases, may work without fee in cases to which they were appointed by the court. The better private-practice lawyers—Carlin's elite of the bar—are usually drawn into criminal work only in those jurisdictions where the court is empowered to select from a list of all practicing attorneys those to be appointed to represent indigent defendants. If the lawyers chosen are reimbursed by the government, it is at a rate usually far below their normal fee schedule. Few like either the meager remuneration or what to them is the hostile atmosphere of criminal court.

"My firm and I would rather have me representing their clients on the more mundane aspects of negligence law at the rate of thirty dollars per hour than do this criminal work for less than ten or fifteen dollars per hour." So Washington, D.C., attorney Thomas M. O'Malley wrote in 1970 in the *D.C. Bar Journal*. In Washington, every law firm and self-employed lawyer of every stratum is called upon occasionally to take an indigent's criminal case for a government-paid fee. "It also is more comforting to work in the friendly atmosphere of one's office than in an unfriendly court where otherwise discerning people sometimes miss the subtle distinctions between the criminal and the defense attorney,"

O'Malley said in his article "My Crime is Being a Lawyer," which called for an end to the random appointment system.

O'Malley further pointed to a possible disadvantage in the system for the defendant, whose appointed lawyer may be a luminary of the local bar but is still likely to be poorly trained for and largely inexperienced in criminal trial work. In appointing lawyers to criminal cases, the courts "don't care what your legal speciality is or how little you know about the criminal law," O'Malley complained. "Persons charged [with crimes] are not being given a fair shake . . . When a substantial defense is presented it is an accident of the system."

In the District of Columbia, each appointed lawyer is, at least, paid by the hour so that his time is fully compensated, albeit at a lower rate than that to which he has become accustomed. In many states and counties, appointed lawyers are paid a flat fee per case ($50 to $100 on the average), no matter how much time they put in and regardless of whether an attorney simply pleads his client guilty or defends him arduously throughout a long trial. The temptation to do as little work as possible in an unfamiliar area of the law or to feel cheated financially for work conscientiously performed is natural.

The President's Commission on Law Enforcement and the Administration of Justice pointed out "Many lawyers in general practice are unwilling to handle criminal matters" and added:

> Criminal business, when it does pay, does not pay well. The lawyer who appears frequently in criminal court runs the risk that the judge will appoint him to serve without compensation in indigent cases. . . .
> Often the lawyer in general practice feels incapable of handling criminal matters skillfully. It is commonly known that criminal courts function under a system of rules and practices familiar only to insiders, which in some cases supercedes the

written codes of criminal procedure. The nonspecialist legitimately doubts his capabilities in the practice of criminal law, a field that received little attention in his formal legal education.

The attorney inexperienced in criminal work may, for instance, insist on a trial for his defendant in a jurisdiction where the judge will penalize the defendant with a much harsher sentence upon conviction than if he had pleaded guilty. Or, on the other hand, the lawyer, knowing about this possibility, may recommend a guilty plea when, unfamiliar with criminal law, he fails to realize that the prosecution's case is too weak to stand up in front of a jury. Experienced prosecutors frequently claim to have outbluffed "uptown" lawyers who come briefly into criminal court to defend zealously but naïvely a client in appointed cases.

"It's like Russian roulette for the defendant," explained a civil lawyer who was appointed frequently to represent indigent criminal defendants for a small government fee in West Virginia. "No one ever knows which lawyers will work hard for that fee or which will just try to plead the man guilty, and no one, including the appointed lawyer himself, knows if he is really competent to try criminal cases."

There are also, in nearly every big-city court, a score or more lawyers who, unlike the reluctant elite of the bar, take only criminal cases. These lawyers, who can be found in or near the criminal courts every day, are always available for judges who may want to turn to them quickly for case appointments rather than try to find a stranger from a distant law office. They are also quite familiar with the criminal-court system. They collect fees when they can from their clients and receive whatever reimbursement the government will give them. Frequently, they wind up representing defendants for nothing or for fees that would seem ludicrously small to a practicing attorney elsewhere.

Unfortunately, however, this informal bar of criminal-court regulars does not provide an acceptable alternative to the appointment of inexperienced elite lawyers to criminal cases. Despite their lengthy criminal-court experience, the regulars are not really the kind of "specialists" in criminal law that the President's Crime Commission called for. The criminal-court regulars are mostly the rejects of their profession, unable to maintain a paying practice any other way. They operate either out of their hats or from cheap, shared offices near the courthouse. They seek out paying clients at the police stations, jails, and arraignment courtrooms—even though such solicitation is prohibited by the rules of legal ethics. In most big-city courts, they can be found wandering the halls, in cheap, loud clothes, seeking clients or trying to arrange a deal with a policeman or prosecutor so that a client already retained or assigned can plead guilty.

The criminal-court regulars are described by the Crime Commission as providing service of "low legal and dubious ethical quality." The Commission's researchers found that

> These lawyers haunt the vicinity of the criminal courts seeking out clients who can pay a modest fee. Some have referral arrangements with bondsmen, policemen or minor court officials. They negotiate guilty pleas and try cases without investigation, preparation, or concern for the particular needs of their clients. Because the prosecution is frequently willing to recommend a light sentence in exchange for a guilty plea in a routine case, the dispositions which these lawyers arrange often appear satisfactory to defendants and other laymen who are ignorant of the fact that the result owes little to the capability of the lawyer.

Most of the capability of these lawyers is directed at collecting whatever fee the defendant can afford. "How much money do you have?" is the first question a new client hears in the court lockup or hallway where he initially meets the lawyer. If it appears to the lawyer that more money can be raised with time, he requests a delay, in consideration of the case, a request which judges seldom deny.

"The lawyer goes out and tries to squeeze money from the defendant's mother or an aunt," explains Judge Charles W. Halleck, of the local trial court in Washington, D.C. "Sometimes, he asks a jailed defendant, 'You got $15 or $25? Here, let me hold it for you.' And later that becomes part of the fee."

Researchers for the President's Crime Commission who watched what goes on during lawyer-defendant interviews inside court lockups saw "defense attorneys demanding from a potential client the loose change in his pocket or the watch on his wrist as a condition of representation." Judge Halleck says, "They don't work if they don't get paid."

"On occasion, defendants have been known to commit additional offenses while at liberty on bail, in order to secure the requisite funds with which to meet their obligations for payment of legal fees," Blumberg notes in his book *Criminal Justice*. "Defense lawyers condition even the most obtuse clients to recognize that there is a firm interconnection between fee payment and the zealous exercise of professional expertise, secret knowledge, and organizational 'connections' on their behalf."

The only real connections the criminal-court regulars have are their bureaucratic ties with everyone else in the courthouse system. If judges help these lawyers along in their fee collection with the approval of a postponement or two, the lawyers can be expected to heed the judges' entreaties that no more time be wasted and as many cases as possible be concluded quickly with guilty pleas. Because the prosecutor is pursuing the same goal, the bargaining between him and the defense lawyer for a plea is not so much determined adversary combat as a mutual desire to strike as quickly as possible a bargain that can be successfully sold to the defendant. "The principals—lawyer and assistant district attorney—rely on one another's cooperation for their continued professional existence," Blumberg found, "and so the bargaining between them tends usually to be 'reasonable' rather than fierce."

Blumberg sees the courthouse defense lawyer in the role of "double agent," who ostensibly represents the interests of the accused, but who winds up representing the interest of the bureaucracy in selling a bargained plea to the defendant. The lawyer is not really independent, as he tries to appear, Blumberg argues, but is actually engaged in "bureaucratic practice, because of the legal practitioner's enmeshment in the authority, discipline, and perspectives of the court organization."

Private legal practice, according to Blumberg, should "involve the maintenance of an organized, disciplined body of knowledge and learning; the individual practitioners are imbued with a spirit of autonomy and service, the earning of a livelihood being incidental." But because the regular criminal-court lawyer, he argues, is "serving higher organizational rather than professional ends, he may be deemed to be engaged in bureaucratic rather than private practice."

The criminal-court regulars do not carry and seldom consult lawbooks. They do not file or argue motions to challenge the prosecution's case, nor do they collect or keep information for their cases. Most of them work simply from well-used datebooks. They avoid taking cases to trial as much out of their own inability to perform before a judge and jury as out of obedience to the pressures of the courthouse bureaucracy. They do not really function as attorneys, but rather as salesmen—slick ones, at that, who often misrepresent their product.

The problem of criminal representation has not been completely overlooked by the legal profession and local governments. The most frequent response to it has been the establishment or expansion of public defender offices. The first ones were opened more than a half century ago, but their growth has been greatest in recent years as appellate courts urged greater recognition of the need for more and better criminal lawyers. There are now more than 100 public defender agencies in the United States, including one in nearly every large city. They range from completely government-supported agencies to nonprofit corporations that receive regular large contributions of public money from local governments, such as the Legal Aid Society in New York City. A few private nonprofit defenders, supported entirely by charity, remain. In no city does the public defender represent all defendants or even all of those who cannot afford to pay a lawyer. Usually, the public defender represents some, the courthouse regulars represent some, and appointed or volunteer private-practice attorneys represent still more. Public defenders are usually salaried and work full time at it. They are selected by the local bar or judges in some cities, by other government officials or by election in other cities.

The vast majority of judges and prosecutors, as Lee Silverstein found, in his three-volume American Bar Foundation study of the representation of low-income criminal defendants, *Defense of the Poor in Criminal Cases in American State Courts*, believe public defenders to be much more capable than the courthouse regulars and more experienced in criminal law than appointed attorneys from the civil bar. There has been increasing talk in many cities of turning over the cases of all indigent defendants to public defenders—and perhaps some of the paying cases as well, with the fee payments helping to reduce the government's share of running the office. But Silverstein also found that many public defenders are already overworked, underpaid, and insufficiently supported by staff.

A more troubling flaw in the public defender concept was

found by David Sudnow, in a series of controlled observations of a big-city public defender office on the West Coast. Sudnow was, at the time, an associate at the Center for the Study of Law and Society at the University of California, Berkeley. The public defenders he watched had become, in his opinion, members of the "core personnel" in the courthouse, who saw the same judges and prosecutors in court day after day and came to think of themselves as part of the government team rather than as adversaries for client interests. They freely expressed their belief that most of their clients were guilty. They tried in their initial interviews with new defendants to force them to admit their guilt and, later, to agree to plead guilty in front of a judge, so as not to waste the court's time or resources. If they found some defendants who they believed were actually innocent, they knew they could usually persuade their prosecutor friends to drop the charges; in turn, they hated to impose on the prosecutor, judge, or themselves the inconvenience of trying cases of defendants who obviously appeared to be guilty. Defendants who insisted on trials in those circumstances were considered "stubborn" cases.

"What the hell are we supposed to do with them?" one public defendant remarked to Sudnow about the problem of stubborn defendants. "If they can't listen to good reason and take a bargain, then it's their tough luck. If they go to prison, well, they're the ones who are losing the trials, not us."

The public defender accepts the court system as it is, despite the cracks that he knows from experience are in it, Sudnow concluded in his study, adding that "The public defender assumes that the D.A., the police, the judge, the narcotics agents and others all conduct their business as it must be conducted. . . ." Police who purjure themselves, judges who abuse their power, laws that discriminate, and court practices that force compromises in place of trials—all of this, says Sudnow, "is taken, as one public defender put it, 'as part of the system and the way it has to be.' And the public defender is part of the team."

Sudnow contended that the public defenders he watched merely went through the motions in trials to avoid being considered negligent in their defense efforts and that the prosecutor could count on the public defender not to test the validity of traditional courthouse procedures or challenge the integrity of the prosecutor's case—by contending, for example, that police witnesses might be lying. In return, the prosecutor would not stage an emotional display designed to inflame the jury against the defendant and would remain open to making last-minute agreements to reduce the charge or the likely sentence in return for a guilty plea. In their conversations with Sudnow, prosecutors and public defenders alike referred to the process as "putting on a trial."

Other observers also have suggested that the public defender might actually be one of the most entrenched of the legal bureaucrats in the trial courts. In interviews, public defenders are rarely willing to attack the system for injustices they recognize as prevalent. They sympathize with other court workers inundated with massive case loads and apologize for the legal short cuts used to cope with the problem. Two studies—Silverstein's which covered several cities, and one by law professors Dallin H. Oaks and Warren Lehman concerning Chicago (*A Criminal Justice System and the Indigent*)—have shown that public defenders are somewhat more likely than private lawyers, including the visiting elite lawyers, to plead their clients guilty and less likely to have the charges against their defendants dismissed. Silverstein's study also showed that the convicted clients of public defenders were sent to prison more often than other convicts. All the researchers pointed out that the public defender usually represents the poorest defendants who are probably less able to help defend themselves. Yet, when cases did go to trial, public defenders showed a higher winning percentage than other types of defense lawyers.

It is important to note that, when speaking about the virtues of the public defender system, most judges begin by pointing out, as did one jurist in an Eastern city's crowded trial court, that public defenders seldom "waste the court's time with frivolous procedural moves and drawn-out trials the way some other lawyers do." The public defender movement is "based as much on the needs of judicial economy as on humanitarian considerations," a group of University of Chicago law students headed by Roger K. Warren contended in a *Chicago Law Review* article in June, 1969, following a study in the criminal court in Cook County, Illinois. "Indeed, when a committee of the Chicago Bar Association summarized the advantages of the recently established Cook County Public Defender in 1931, it emphasized the expeditious handling of court matters," they reported and noted that the then Public Defender of Cook County had reaffirmed in his most recent annual report his view that his office had remedied "a chaotic situation in the administration and disposition of cases." Judges and prosecutors prefer the public defender to private lawyers, the Chicago law students suggested, because they are more pleased "by his success in efficiently handling heavy case-loads than by his success in representing an indigent defendant."

"Today's cure-all is the public defender," Dan H. McCullough, a past president of the National Association of Defense Lawyers, wrote in the *American Bar Association Journal*. But, from his experience, he concluded:

> I just cannot bring myself to believe that the tough, hard job of the defense of one charged with a crime can be done by a bureaucrat . . . Often the lawyer is required to fly in the face of public opinion. I just can't see the public defender defend-

ing the little individual. He is more likely in company with his opposite bureaucratic number, the prosecutor, to sweep another mistake under the rug.

But today there are few independent criminal lawyers like McCullough. As he himself points out, his is a rare, vanishing breed. Mostly, there are just the hack courthouse regulars.

The defense lawyer's "opposite bureaucratic number, the prosecutor" is no more likely to be a well-trained, experienced, independent-thinking lawyer working singlemindedly to produce justice. Often, the trial court prosecutor is a young man just out of law school, with the one standard course in criminal law behind him and little or no on-the-job instruction. He is pushed out into the courtroom and left to sink or swim as each case is called and he must decide which the government should prosecute and which it should drop and then try those cases that remain. Usually, the young man has taken the job to gain trial experience. Within a few years, at about the time he has become experienced and proficient in his work, he is likely to take his skills into private law practice for double or triple his meager government salary.

The nation's criminal courts in effect are legal training laboratories for young prosecutors, and the persons involved in each case are their guinea pigs. Over and over again across the country, one comes upon a criminal-courtroom scene in which a judge is carefully leading an inexperienced prosecutor through the motions of a hearing or trial and prodding him to ask questions and raise objections at the proper times. Sometimes, the judge must phrase particularly important questions for the prosecutor, suggest arguments he should make, remind him of routine points of criminal procedure, and instruct him in such basic courtroom techniques as standing far away from a witness while asking questions so that the witness, in attempting to answer the distant prosecutor, will talk loudly enough for everyone in court to hear.

Thus, in New York City's Criminal Court, a young prosecutor having difficulty trying the government's case against a school teacher charged with disorderly conduct during a local sit-in protest, got a lot of help from the judge. Plainly realizing that important civil liberties questions were involved and that the case would probably be appealed if the defendant were convicted, the judge was taking pains to have everything run right. At one point, as the defense lawyer from the American Civil Liberties Union, who was developing his case expertly, carefully questioned an important witness, the judge turned his head to the prosecutor and looked at him expectantly. He got no response.

"Mr. Gibbs?" the judge then called out.

"Uh . . . objection, your honor," the prosecutor responded, the confusion on his face making clear that he did not know why he should be objecting or what his objection was.

"Objection sustained," the judge ruled.

A few moments later, as the questioning continued, the judge turned again and stared hard at the prosecutor, this time catching his eye.

"Objection, your honor," the prosecutor said, jumping to his feet.

"Sustained," the judge responded.

It was evident to everybody in the court (with the possible exception of the muddled young man) that the judge felt that the defense attorney's questioning had gotten out of bounds. But he wanted to have the record show that the prosecutor had expressed doubt about it, as a prosecutor should, and that he, the judge, was merely responding, as a judge should. Later, with the case drawing to a close, it was necessary for the judge to remind the prosecutor of motions he should have made. The judge also had to explain the correct way to make some of these motions and how to respond in turn to procedural moves of the defense.

In a Cleveland courtroom, another young prosecutor kept asking a complaining witness the wrong questions, which led to answers having nothing to do with the case at hand. Finally, the prosecutor was waved into silence by the exasperated judge, who then questioned the witness himself. In Washington, D.C., a judge, trying without a jury the case of a landlord charged with willful violations of the housing code, had to dictate to the prosecutor, word for word, the argument he should make in contending that the landlord was guilty. Then, after the prosecutor repeated it back to him, the judge ruled, affirmatively, on his own contention.

Not only the young prosecutor but also the young prosecutor's boss—called the district attorney, state's attorney, or chief prosecutor, depending on the local jurisdiction—often is just as poorly trained for his job. He is usually elected or appointed from a group of political party contenders, none of whom possess much background for the job. Usually, he intends to serve only for a relatively short period of time and looks upon the position primarily as a steppingstone in a political career.

The President's Crime Commission found that only four state court systems and the federal system provide for the appointment of prosecutors, and even in these jurisdictions partisan considerations appear to play a vital part in their selection. Although in a few communities highly competent men have made a career in the office, in most places the incumbent moves on after one or two terms. These men go on to higher elective office or, if unsuccessful in later politics, they return to the more lucrative private law practice from which they came.

The majority of the elected prosecutors are chosen on the

basis of political. acumen rather than legal qualifications. Generally, they are men who had previously been practicing civil law and working in party politics. Most have not had any sustained contact with criminal law since that lone law school course on the subject, and they are, if anything, even less knowledgeable about it than a recent graduate. Inevitably, each man spends much of his time in office merely learning the system, rather than challenging or trying to surmount it. All the while, he finds his office inundated with work but shortchanged in budget and staff.

In addition, the Crime Commission noted, "political ambition does not encourage a prosecutor to take the risks that frequently inhere in reasoned judgments." Guilty pleas, for instance, do produce a high conviction rate—even if they are convictions without trials and frequently for charges quite different than the crime committed, so that lenient sentences can be given in exchange for the pleas. More trials could mean more acquittals and certainly would lead to even longer delays in court, both of which might make the prosecutor unpopular.

Moreover, in all but the largest cities, the prosecutor's pay is so comparatively low for the legal profession that many prosecutors carry on at least part of their old private law practices on the side. The law usually allows this practice, which not only presents opportunities for possible conflicts of interest but also drains away that energy and dedication the prosecutor needs to bring to his performance if he is to do more than merely hammer out guilty pleas.

In many ways, the prosecutor can be even more important in the criminal-court system than the judge. It is the prosecutor who decides which defendants will be tried and which nine of every ten trial-bound cases will be ended instead by guilty pleas. It is the prosecutor who acts on behalf of the public in these negotiations and, in most jurisdictions, also gives the bargain final approval. The judge merely rubber-stamps the agreement in court. But, although they cannot realistically be expected to be very much more competent or dedicated than the prosecutors or district attorneys and the lawyers who practice before them, it should not be concluded that the judges themselves are unimportant in either criminal or civil courtrooms.

Often, it is the judge alone who can determine whether or not justice is done in his courtroom. He tries many cases himself and guides juries through others. He rules on what witnesses can or cannot say. He shapes issues to be decided and instructs juries on how the law applies to them. He decides what the lawyers before him can or cannot say and do. He can bring considerable pressure on opposing lawyers to reach compromise settlements of cases short of trial. He sentences criminal defendants. Most importantly, perhaps, he sets the tone of proceedings—rushed or deliberate, serious or farcical, fair or prejudicial. Much of what the trial judge says or does is within his sole discretion and cannot be overruled by appeal to higher courts.

"In the long run," the late Supreme Court Justice Benjamin Cardozo wrote, "there is no guarantee of justice except the personality of the judge."

Thus, it is a bad sign, to say the least, that all too often the trial judge's personality is a cause for alarm. Many judges this writer observed in trial courts throughout the country showed a marked and disturbing lack of what lawyers call "judicial temperament"—the ability to restrain one's emotions and set an example of integrity for others, to avoid abuse of the awesome power accorded to the man wearing the black robe inside the courtroom, and to act always in the interest of justice rather than to satisfy personal whim or prejudice. There are many judges in many places who depart from this ideal in ways ranging from laughable impropriety to ruthless arrogance, which undermines respect for the court, and, even worse, vengefulness that does serious harm to citizens in the name of the law.

A judge in Texas, conducting a murder trial involving persons connected with the University of Texas, instructed Percy Foreman, the noted criminal lawyer, to use the phrase "University of Texas, Number One" any time he referred to the college. The judge, a former University of Texas law student, was a fan of the college's football team, which had been acclaimed as the country's best by wire-service polls and President Richard Nixon after an undefeated season in 1969.

A judge conducting arraignments of routine criminal cases in Cleveland, Ohio, kept up a continual stream of degrading remarks about black citizens who came before his bench. Of a strapping young man accused of fighting with a policeman, the judge said with mock fright, "I'd certainly hate to run into that in a dark alley." As a full-figured black woman wearing a short skirt and filmy blouse walked away from the bench after being arraigned on a charge of performing obscenely as an exotic dancer, the judge whistled softly and addressed a loud, grinning aside to the prosecutor, "Stacked, isn't she?"

A Maryland judge who sentenced a fifty-three-year-old black woman to eight years in prison for the knifing of a relative in an argument although both the prosecutor and the defense lawyer had urged that she be placed on probation, dismissed their pleas with the remark, "If they want to live like animals, let them stay in pens."

In some courtrooms, judges bored with the tedium of accident injury suits appeared to doze, stare blankly into space, or read during testimony. Judges who tired under the pressure of heavy calendars of criminal or traffic cases became rude and abusive to the citizens who came before them. Some cut off lawyers in midsentence and ruled on

legal questions before the attorneys were given an opportunity. Others simply did not appear competent to discharge
their responsibilities fully. The police court judge in Cleveland who insulted Negroes in his courtroom managed, during two days of observation, to avoid making definitive legal
rulings on most of the criminal cases that came before him.
He sent all serious cases, the felony charges, to the grand
jury without the requisite full hearing in his courtroom and
referred both the complainant and defendant in minor cases,
such as husband-and-wife fights, barroom brawls, and lar-
cenies, to the probation office "to talk things over." A judge
in Washington, D.C., deferred so much of his courtroom
work to his clerk that, one day, while the judge left the
bench to answer the telephone without his clerk's knowledge, the clerk decided eighty-seven landlord and tenant
cases while the bench behind him was empty. In city after
city, judges were observed having difficulty ruling on routine
legal points or making mistakes that appeared obvious to a
layman and often angered the lawyers involved.

More frequently, however, trial court judges appeared to
be neither incompetent nor intemperate so much as content
merely to put in minimal, mindlessly bureaucratic effort.
They usually failed to explain fully to each defendant his
rights, as required by U.S. Supreme Court decisions. They
accepted guilty pleas without questioning how these pleas
were negotiated, or they did little to improve the quality of
rushed trials. The judges who called each day's dockets of
cases and logged the postponements seemed more interested
in the calendar than in justice; their biggest concern was
finding another date to which each postponed case could
quickly be continued so that the next case could be called.
When two lawyers in New York City agreed to continue a
certain criminal case on a future date, the judge, calendar
in hand, reminded them that the date they chose was a
Jewish holiday, in case it mattered to them. "You see," the

judge explained with some pride, "I've got a calendar here with all the holidays on it. I know every holiday in the year."

According to Columbia University law professor Maurice Rosenberg, "A judge need not be vicious, corrupt or witless to be a menace in office. Mediocrity can be in the long run as much a pollutant as venality, for it dampens opposition and is more likely to be tolerated." Yet mediocrity is almost assured for our trial judges by the system that produces them. By popular election or political appointment, they are winnowed from the few lawyers willing to give up lucrative private practices for the electoral uncertainty, low salary, and high pressure of the trial court bench. The process occasionally turns up an exceptional man who wants to make the sacrifice, but more often a trial court judgeship appeals only to those pedestrian practitioners who were not destined to do very well in private practice or who believe that election as a judge could be the first step to higher office. Furthermore, the man elected judge usually comes from a rather narrow private practice of one sort or another, and he is given no refresher course in the many other areas of the law he will encounter on the bench. Nor is he provided any training for the special responsibilities of being a judge.

There is also a tendency on everybody's part to seek the better available lawyers for appellate court judgeships and relegate those with primarily political qualifications to the lower trial courts. "When and how can it be brought home to the legal profession and to the public generally that a man worthy by character and temperament to be an appellate judge is, in a real sense, even more unworthy to be entrusted with the highly visible powers and responsibilities of a trial judge?" asks Columbia professor Harry W. Jones in his *The Law, The Courts and the Population Explosion*.

"The true judgemakers," the President's Crime Commission concluded, "are the leaders of the dominant [political] party," who select the candidates for local judgeships. As the commission described it,

> The process of selection is apt to be carried on in private meetings. Intricate bargaining patterns may evolve in which certain political leaders will assert dominion over certain judgeships, and balances must be struck to reward the party's financial supporters or those who have labored for the party organization. All too frequently in this bargaining process scant attention is given to the abilities of the proposed candidates.

"It is practically impossible for the public, especially in large centers of population, to know anything about the qualifications for judicial office of those who practice at the bar," according to Judge Samuel I. Rosenman of New York. Writing in the *Journal of the American Judicature Society* in 1964, Judge Rosenman added:

> The voters, as a whole, know little more about the candidates than what their campaign picture may reveal . . . Their concern is centered on the executive and legislative candidates because they are identified with the only issues and causes which interest the voters.

A poll made in New York State just after the 1954 election showed what scant concern the voter has for who is to be a judge. Three of every five voters had paid no attention to the judicial candidates before the election, and, within ten days after the election, four of every five could not name even one they had voted for.

Once elected, the judge does not necessarily have to compile a particularly distinguished judicial record to keep his seat on the bench. But he must maintain strong political ties, so as not to lose his party's support. He must himself contribute to the party's coffers and in turn solicit contributions for his re-election campaign—often from the lawyers who practice in front of him in court. "I learned at first hand what it means for a judicial candidate to have to seek votes in political club houses," complained Judge Rosenman of his several election campaigns during nearly four decades on the bench, "to ask for the support of political district leaders, to receive financial contributions from lawyers and others, and to make speeches about his own qualifications to audiences who could not care less." Each year in Chicago when Mayor Richard Daley is up for re-election, many judges of the Cook County trial bench sport Daley buttons on their lapels.

In some states, the election of judges is nonpartisan. In this case, the bar associations usually pick the most popular (which is not to say necessarily the most able) of their number to run. Under this system, the voters are still not well informed about judicial qualifications. In fact, the American Judicature Society has declared that a nonpartisan judicial election may be the worst method of all because it is likely to put on the bench the candidate "having the same name as a well-known public figure, a large campaign fund, a pleasing TV image, or the proper place on the ballot."

Neither partisan nor nonpartisan election of judges seems to work out well, the President's Crime Commission observed, adding:

> A lawyer with a good private practice may be unwilling to curry the favor of the politicians or to undertake a personal campaign in order to get his name placed on the ballot. When a sitting judge has to run for reelection, he must take time off from his work to campaign. In closely contested elections campaign expenses can be substantial, and the sense of obligation that a successful candidate incurs to his financial supporters may strain his vow of impartiality . . . It is [also] possible that a judge who must shortly stand for reelection may be unduly influenced by what he conceives to be the popular view of how a case should be decided.

One alternative to elections is executive appointment of judges. Governors or state legislators perform this duty in several states, most in New England. In many others where judicial elections are held, the governor is also empowered to fill suddenly vacated judgeships until the next regular election. But few observers argue that the appointment process produces judges of any higher caliber than do elections. Many governors treat judgeships as patronage jobs. They either reward defeated officeholders for their party loyalty or respond to pressures from local party bosses in selecting judges for trial courts in their jurisdictions.

The only other judicial selection method used in the United States today is the Missouri Plan, adopted in that state in 1940 and championed ever since by court reformers. It provides for a nonpartisan, unpaid panel of an equal number of lawyers chosen by the bar association and laymen picked by the governor, which recommends candidates for a judicial vacancy. The nominating commission places advertisements in the newspapers and inquiries with the bar associations to come up with a broad sample of prospective candidates, from which three names are recommended for each vacancy. The Missouri governor has usually satisfied reformers with his selections from the list of commission nominees; among other factors, judges from both parties have always been selected. At the next general election occurring more than one year after appointment, the judge then goes before the voters without opposition on the ballot for approval. The vote is a yes-or-no decision on whether the judge should be retained in office. If he should be voted out, the original selection process would be used to pick a successor.

This scheme is now used for state appellate courts and Saint Louis and Kansas City county courts in Missouri and for some significant judicial offices in Iowa, Kansas, and Nebraska. Only in Alaska are all judges of higher trial courts selected by the Missouri Plan. In California, Illinois, and Michigan, sitting judges are all originally appointed or elected to the bench by traditional methods but stand for re-election on a Missouri-style ballot to be voted up or down without opposition.

Although the Missouri Plan seems to be the best yet devised for placing higher-quality lawyers on the bench, it, too, has inherent drawbacks. The re-election process is such that the voters, without being given a choice between two men, are unlikely to vote out the sitting judge unless they are especially displeased with him. (In Missouri, no sitting judge has yet been voted out of office under the plan in three decades.) A proven thief might be defeated, but a dangerously mediocre judge may well remain in office. Until a foolproof selection process is found, it is safe to say that a community usually will get the caliber of judges it actively seeks.

Just as important as the selection process—perhaps more so—are two other considerations: how new judges are trained for their work and whether those judges who do not perform well can be removed from the bench.

Special training for judges is virtually nonexistent. A judge is never required to train himself, and only a comparative handful go voluntarily to weekend or week-long national or state judicial training conferences (a relatively new phenomenon, which too often provides more folksy speeches and socializing than practical instruction). The National College of State Trial Judges runs an impressive month-long training course, but it is attended at great expense by only a very small fraction of the nation's new jurists each year.

The newly selected judge is likely to be out of touch with important legal developments outside his special field of practice. Many new judges, for instance, have had almost no criminal-trial experience at all. More importantly, having been an advocate, the lawyer becoming a judge has had no experience or training in the most critical tasks a judge must perform: deciding cases rather than merely arguing one side of them, instructing and managing a jury, sentencing convicted criminal defendants, administering court business. The new judge usually learns all this by trial and error, while deciding civil and criminal cases that greatly influence the lives of others.

The late Supreme Court Justice Felix Frankfurter once argued that any good lawyer improves when he puts on a judge's gown. But Harry W. Jones has countered by pointing out that bad lawyers may well be *worse* as judges and should not be expected magically to grow in stature if named to the bench. "Nowhere in the whole range of public office," Jones contends, "are weaknesses of character, intellect, or psychic constitution revealed more mercilessly than in the discharge of the responsibilities of a trial judge."

The pressures and responsibilities of judging make it imperative that some way be found to remove those judges who prove to be the wrong men for the job, who never train themselves thoroughly in its intricacies, or who, though once capable, have grown feeble or ill and refuse to give up their seats on the bench. Some states try to make retirement so financially attractive (compared to the moderate working salary) that a judge will incline to step down at the slightest urging. But, in most states, a recall election on a petition from the voters or impeachment by the legislature are the only methods of forcing a judge out. These methods have thus far proven too unwieldy for weeding out the incapacitated, misbehaving, or incompetent.

California has a judicial-removal commission that investigates all complaints from citizens and lawyers against state judges. It can issue warnings to judges and petition the state supreme court to remove them. Dozens of judges have complied with its warnings, and thirty have either been removed from office or, more frequently, resigned as a result of commission complaints. The California commission is still a subject of some controversy, however, among the state's jurists, who fear it can be used to carry out citizen vendettas against them. No other state has so powerful a watchdog over the judiciary. A few state supreme courts have the power to remove trial judges from the bench, but they seldom take such action and they have no supporting agency to investigate and act regularly on every complaint about judges, as the California commission does.

To a layman such as this writer, who has reported on and immersed himself in the day-to-day problems of the courts, several changes seem necessary if the over-all quality of service is to improve. Because lawyers and judges alike in the trial court bureaucracy continue to remain outside the mainstream of legal activity and unresponsive to the needs of the public and the ideals of justice, reorganization of the legal profession itself—from law school to the judge's bench —is imperative.

To begin with, every law student could be taught, in his first years, more about the skills required in trial court, criminal law, the legal problems of the poor, and the conditions that actually exist in trial courts. More law schools could—as only a very few now do—send students for a summer or a semester to work inside the trial courts as helpers to public defenders and poverty lawyers or as researchers for those studying the problems of the courts. This study and experience would better prepare all law school graduates for some service in the trial courts and open their eyes to the shortcomings of the courts, and this experience would, in turn, surely incline them to urge reforms. Then, with this broader background behind them, law students could specialize in any area of law practice they choose in their third, and, if necessary, fourth, year in school. They should still be required to maintain some contact with the trial courts, however, during at least one summer or semester of their later school years.

The next step would be a required legal internship of a

year or two for every law school graduate before he can hang out his shingle—much as doctors and dentists must serve a supervised and socially beneficial internship before becoming licensed to practice. Just as the future doctor must spend time interning for the public good, as well as for his own benefit, in the general hospital, budding lawyers should all intern in the trial courts or their supporting services. They should work with older lawyers and other professionals in the prosecutor's office, public defender agencies, poverty law offices, probation departments, and the like. Such a program would increase the woefully inadequate manpower in these fields and provide a way for prospective lawyers to be trained in the trial courts without learning on their own at the expense of the public. It might also serve, if combined with higher starting salaries in the trial courts, to attract some of the more able interns to full-time court work. And an influx of still idealistic young interns and lawyers into the trial courts could help break down the bureaucratic bulwark against change. The law school curriculum also should include some course work in other disciplines, such as psychology, medicine, and the life sciences; these are becoming increasingly important in the work of our trial courts, which today deal with large questions of mental illness and criminality, product liability, and the like.

Meaningful graduate and continuing education programs could be offered, too, in such legal specialties as the role of the trial judge or in advanced criminal or consumer law, both of which are important in trial court work. Criminal lawyers and public defenders could be required to earn an advanced degree or credits in criminal law before being allowed to try cases of more serious offenses. All lawyers who wish to become judges should be required to take as much as a year of formal advanced study of the judge's role in court either before or after they are nominated, but certainly before they are allowed to ascend to the bench. Such advanced courses would include contact with the trial courts themselves and their everyday problems.

The law schools also could provide a shorter course of perhaps a year leading to certification of subprofessionals in trial court work, such as clerks and probation officers. This single law school year could follow courses in modern management for prospective clerks and college degrees in sociology or psychology for probation officers.

Each lawyer going into a special practice that touches the public should also be required to earn some certification in that specialty through advanced training and experience. The certification would provide assurance for the client, who now has none but the lawyer's salesmanship, that he is qualified to try a divorce, accident injury, consumer complaint, or criminal case. There is no reason, of course, why similar certification in special fields should not be required of lawyers in corporate, tax, or government practice.

Finally, every state and suitable political subdivision should have commissions composed of both laymen and lawyers to supervise the disciplining of practicing attorneys, to screen candidates for judicial nominations, and to investigate complaints against judges. The commissions should be well known to the public and investigate with professional staff all complaints against lawyers and judges. In cases in which the complaint is unjustified or a private warning suffices to ensure compliance with the law, rules of legal ethics, and specified standards of judicial performance, the commission could act confidentially, reporting these actions only in secret upon request to the state or local governing body, as a check on the commission's fidelity. All censures and disbarments of lawyers and recommendations of removal of judges should be widely publicized, however, to discourage potential wrongdoers.

Serious breaches of legal ethics that are not also law violations should be punishable within the legal profession by fines paid into a fund to compensate client-victims of attorneys' misconduct. All practicing lawyers should also contribute to these funds, which could purchase group malpractice insurance for further protection of clients and for the attorneys themselves.

None of these suggestions will come as startling ones to the legal profession. A Florida judge and a San Francisco lawyer have proposed variations of legal internships in law review articles. The Georgetown University Law School, with the financial help of the Ford Foundation, now runs a quite sophisticated graduate program of study and intern work in both criminal and civil law in the trial courts of Washington, D.C. Several law schools send students to local courts as lawyers' helpers during summers. Many other law students work on their own as clerks to trial court judges while studying. Judges' groups have been sponsoring training conferences for new judges that grow nearly every year in breadth and formality, although they still are attended by a very tiny fraction of the nation's judges.

At this time, however, the legal profession seems unlikely to commit itself to a complete overhaul of its schooling and professional structure. It would mean a sharp break with tradition and a kind of bending to the dictates of public concern that most lawyers hate to do. The mere suggestion of placing laymen on discipline committees affecting members of that most exclusive of American men's clubs, the bar, has always brought about instant and fierce lawyer resistance—and this despite the ironic fact that lawyers every day draw up legislation that puts increasing numbers of other professionals under varying degrees of public accountability and control.

It will remain up to the public, then, to insist that lawyers do something about the cynical bureaucracy of the trial courts and, in the bargain, improve the profession's conduct and service to the public. To do so with any degree of success, the public must itself be willing to pay higher salaries for trial court personnel, to finance legal internships, perhaps to subsidize law schools—and, most importantly, to increase greatly the attention it now pays to the trial courts and the energy it expends to work for their reform. All this is a hard thing to put one's mind to before being served a summons or called to jury duty—but, if American justice is to become viable, such diligence is an absolute essential.

VIII

To Re-Establish Justice:
Making the Law Work

"Something is very wrong in America," New York Mayor John V. Lindsay observed in an April, 1970, speech. "What has happened to the Rule of Law in America?"

Lindsay was referring to the lawlessness in U.S. cities that threatens to become epidemic, to the dissatisfied minorities in American society who engage in disruption and guerrilla warfare, and to the panicky citizenry that seems to be increasingly tolerant of repressive police action against criminals and dissenters alike.

Who would argue with the mayor that something is very wrong? Too many city streets, deserted by the mainstream of society, have become armed camps, where police, thieves, merchants who carry guns in their belts, and roving guerrilla snipers periodically open fire on each other. Hundreds of businesses and buildings, from ghetto storefronts to Manhattan offices and college classrooms across the country, have been burned and bombed. Police and national guardsmen club young demonstrators, shoot rioters and looters in the back, and fire into unarmed crowds. An alarming number of good people have gone along with the violence on one side or the other—excusing urban terrorism in the name of revolution or cheering a U.S. Vice-President's call for increased repression of dissenters while keeping loaded guns in their automobiles and bedroom nightstands.

Fewer and fewer Americans seem to be obeying the law or putting their faith in it as an answer to the lawlessness of others or a means to assuage the anguish of social injustice. At a time when critical problems appear to be confronting them in greater volume than ever before, they are overwhelmed by a frightening erosion of that stabilizing influence, which as a people they have counted on since the nation's beginning: the Rule of Law.

What has happened?

The Constitution and the Bill of Rights were intended to guarantee that justice and liberty would prevail regardless of the tests the nation might be put to. Citizens were expected to rely on the law rather than take up violent means to achieve even urgent social ends. The nation continued to maintain reasonable faith in the Rule of Law even when legal and political institutions did not seem to be working so well, and it avoided a complete breakdown during such difficult and different periods as the rapid and chaotic frontier expansion, the violence-marred struggles to establish trade unionism, the corruption of Prohibition days, the desperation of the Great Depression, the paranoia of McCarthyism and earlier know-nothing political reactions, and the stresses of foreign wars.

"The law, the working of the law, the daily application of the law to people and situations, is an essential element in a country's life," author Sybille Bedford observed in her international study of legal institutions, *The Faces of Justice.* "It runs through everything; it is part of the pattern like the architecture and the art and the look of the cultivated countryside. It shapes and expresses a country's mode of thought, its political concepts and realities, its conduct."

As long as Americans assumed that justice and individual

freedom were ultimately protected by the way the law worked, their faith in the rule of law was not seriously shaken. But that assumption began some time ago to clash rudely with reality in the cities, as the crowded courts became increasingly unable to dispense daily justice to those who came before them. This problem has grown much worse and begun to affect a much larger proportion of the population.

"Impressed with a conviction that the true administration of justice is the firmest pillar of good government," George Washington said, "I have considered the first arrangement of the judicial department as essential to the happiness of our country and the stability of its political system."

Overburdened, undermanned, and backward in operation, the nation's trial courts some two hundred years later barely survive as bureaucratic institutions. They are failing to cope with widespread disregard for the law or with the inequities in American society that flout the meaning of justice as the increasing frustration experienced every day by the hundreds of thousands who come into contact with them undermines general respect for and trust in the law.

American businessmen have turned their backs on the trial courts, former New York appellate judge David Peck pointed out some time ago in a bar journal admonition to fellow judges and lawyers. "Until the late 1920's, the courts were principally occupied with commercial litigation," he noted. "Today, commercial litigation has all but left the courts."

"Disappointed and disgusted" with courthouse inefficiency and incompetence, "the procedural rigmarole and the slow and cumbersome trial process," the businessmen pulled out of the court, "engaged in self-help and created their own tribunals and procedures for handling cases," Peck recounted. "Now, sixty trade associations in this country maintain arbitration tribunals which handle most of the commercial cases . . . largely without benefit of lawyers." Or the courts.

Government, too, as it began new programs for social security, workmen's compensation, welfare benefits, business subsidies, and the like built into each its own system for adjudicating disputes, complaints, and inequities—to avoid the chaotic courts. "Let us make no mistake about it," Peck warned the bench and bar. "The same practices which have driven commercial litigation from the courts operate adversely on the litigation which remains and threaten similarly to drive it from the courts and the [legal] profession."

The most numerous users of the trial courts today are ordinary citizens: crime victims, witnesses, and accused criminals; traffic offenders, automobile accident victims, and accident witnesses; landlords and tenants; merchants and creditors trying to collect unpaid debts; wronged consumers; divorcing couples; heirs to estates; citizens involved in common disputes with other citizens. These people, as Peck explained, "seek simplicity and economy of procedure, expertise in the consideration and expedition in the disposition of cases."

But what they are faced with instead are interminable delays, the necessity for countless return trips, expensive legal fees, and poorly trained and frequently uncaring judges, lawyers, and clerks, who do little to make the courts responsive to the needs of the public. Justice is callously denied them daily—causing inconvenience, hardship, and worse for most who come into contact with the courts. No wonder that many are today convinced that the law does not work for them.

In his extraordinary "state of the judiciary" speech to the American Bar Association in August, 1970, and in more detail later in a lengthy interview in *U.S. News and World Report* (December 14, 1970), Chief Justice Warren E. Burger of the U.S. Supreme Court expressed fear that the legal system's many problems could destroy "the sense of confidence in the courts [that] is essential to maintain the fabric of ordered liberty for a free people." He warned that citizens are coming to believe that "the system isn't protecting the public from crime," that "inefficiency and delay will drain even a just [court] judgment of its value" because "five or six years after you've broken your leg or damaged your automobile is too long to wait for a recovery," and that "the courts cannot vindicate the legal rights . . . exploited in the smaller transactions of daily life [concerning] home appliances, repairs, finance charges, and the like."

It is not surprising then to see all around us ominous signs that Peck's prediction is beginning to come true—that the average American who is the primary client of the trial courts is turning his back on them. More and more often, victims of crime and traffic accidents, witnesses, wronged consumers, and others—especially those who have been there before—avoid going to court if they can, even if not going means letting a criminal go free or turning down the chance to have a financial loss compensated.

Many of them know that the end result of persevering through the chaotic trial court process usually is an unsatisfactory compromise, in which after everybody's trouble the criminal goes free, anyway, or the amount realized from a civil suit of many years' duration adds up, after legal fees, to only a fraction of the loss originally suffered. Lawbreakers laugh at the impotence of the courts, while those citizens seeking redress before the law for suffering as victims of crimes, discrimination, or economic exploitation become embittered about the courts' failure to assure them safety and justice. Criminals feel free to strike again. The deprived and oppressed feel compelled to disrupt society with violence. Those who feel threatened by these forces angrily ready themselves to strike back however they can.

Not that all this is new. The problems in our courts have long been recognized but have gone untreated. Roscoe

Pound, the Nebraska lawyer who later became America's foremost legal educator and advocate of court reform, warned in 1906 that U.S. courts worked so badly that they caused "popular dissatisfaction with the administration of justice." The daily experience of injustice, delay, and expense had created, Pound said in a landmark address to the American Bar Association, "a deep-seated desire to keep out of court, right or wrong, on the part of every sensible businessman in the community."

The problems grew worse as the years passed, affecting others besides businessmen. In 1913, Pound concluded in a *Harvard Law Review* article on urban justice that the

> courts in our great cities . . . are subjected to almost overwhelming pressure by an accumulated mass of litigation. Usually they sit almost the year round, and yet they tire out parties and witnesses with long delays, and . . . dispose of . . . business so hastily or imperfectly that reversals and retrials are continually required.

In 1921, Pound found in a study of criminal courts in Cleveland that "the professional criminal and his advisers have learned rapidly to use this machinery and make devices intended to temper the application of criminal law to the occasional offender a means of escape for the habitual offender." He also saw, in the Cleveland of the 1920's, chaotic court organization, inept judges, haggling lawyers, and poor treatment of the public. All survive—and grow worse—in Cleveland and elsewhere today.

Through the next several decades, study after study followed those Pound had made, culminating in the massive survey of modern American courts by the prestigious President's Commission on Law Enforcement and the Administration of Justice in 1965 and 1966. Its final report said:

> The Commission has been shocked by what it has seen in some lower courts . . . It has seen cramped and noisy courtrooms,

undignified and perfunctory procedures, and badly trained personnel. It has seen dedicated people who are frustrated by huge caseloads, by the lack of opportunity to examine cases carefully, and by the impossibility of devising constructive solutions to the problems of offenders. It has seen assembly line justice.

As time passed, the nagging problems of big-city courts were exacerbated greatly by rapid population growth and social change. In addition to being inundated with many more serious crimes, the archaic court system also began to be beset with fast-rising numbers of cases involving such practices as narcotics addiction, alcoholism, gambling, and divorce. The automobile also loosed an avalanche of litigation for which the courts were ill prepared. Finally, the courts began to be asked more often to find legal answers to pressing problems of poverty, discrimination, economic exploitation, and despoliation of the environment.

The world changed rapidly. But our trial courts stayed the same, and, as they became more and more overloaded, they failed to assign priorities for their limited resources. They also remained manned largely by hack lawyers and political warhorse judges, who today have increasing difficulty coping with the conflicts of society that have been visited on the trial courts. Thus, all the shortcomings that first raised serious concern at the beginning of this century have now multiplied and intensified, leaving the trial courts themselves on the verge of collapse at a time when they are critically needed to help forestall general urban—and possibly national—collapse.

In spite of the evidence of many, many studies and what the eye can see and the ear hear, the American legal profession by and large has consistently refused to admit that our courts need reforming as badly as they do. There is still **widespread lip service paid by lawyers to what Jerome**

Frank, the late appellate judge and eloquent champion of court reform, in his book *Courts on Trial,* called the "justice myths." From generation to generation, lawyers passed on "stork stories," as Frank called them, about the origins of the American legal system. Lawyers have characterized as an almost divine heritage that which really evolved haphazardly from the eighteenth-century English countryside. They argue, in effect, that our basic court structure and procedures are somehow too sacred to be changed radically. They fight suggestions for sweeping reform with more tenacity, and thus far more success, than did American doctors who tried to counteract the public's demand for government-paid medical care.

Part of the reason for this disregard for the public good is that many leading lawyers have not been inside local trial courts for years. As noted earlier, they work in commerce or government or practice at the bars of higher appellate courts and do not realize how quickly the lower courts are deteriorating. Many younger lawyers who still must frequent the halls of the lower courts are too preoccupied with getting out of them to spend time and effort at reform, while the few who do try are soon discouraged by the treadmill and the refusal of influential local bar leaders to back them up.

Large numbers of lawyers and other citizens also retain the mistaken notion that the workings of the lower courts are subject to close regulation by the appellate courts. They believe that anything that goes wrong in the trial courts can be righted on appeal and that the major problems plaguing trial courts must be the result of misguided appellate court rulings. This "upper court myth," as Frank called it, may be the most damaging of all. It fails to recognize that the appellate courts review only a tiny fraction of lower court cases and that the sample is badly distorted because most trial court business is transacted through compromise in ultimately untried cases, the mechanics of which never receive appellate review. Thus, the wheeling and dealing and the raw conditions of the lower courts are ignored in legal and public debate, as well as in legal education and study for reform. There is instead a preoccupation with controversial Supreme Court decisions on the right of an accused criminal to have a lawyer, the admissibility of confessions and other evidence, and similar subjects. Actually, such decisions affect less than 1 per cent of the work of the lower courts.

Judges and lawyers also have vested interests in maintaining the *status quo* in our trial courts. Many judges like their autonomy, their short working hours and special privileges, despite the confusion and injustice all around them. The courthouse bureaucrats, themselves harried by the troublesome conditions, nevertheless resist intrusion by outsiders; the questionable methods the regulars have devised for coping with the overloaded calendar constitute the only way they know of keeping a finger in the dike, and they are not about to pull it out to test someone else's theories. Finally, there are tens of thousands of lawyers whose livelihood depends on the kinds of litigation that reformers would like to remove from the overcrowded courts, such as automobile accident claims, divorce, the prosecution of habitual gamblers and prostitutes.

But it is also true that, when someone from the legal community does raise a call of alarm, not only other lawyers but also nearly everybody else responds with dismaying apathy. American taxpayers simply do not support their courts. They pay less to run the criminal courts than for any other part of the crime control system. National concern about crime and disorder has produced large increases in local and federal support for police forces—tens of thousands of new policemen with helicopters, computers, advanced communications systems, and other wonders of the age—but almost nothing for the courts. Criminals are caught but not tried. Some city courts are still expected to operate largely on the money they collect in fines. The choosing of judges and clerks to run the courts usually devolves on officeholders who pick political cronies or voters who blindly rubber-stamp the candidates of party bosses.

We cannot leave the trial courts to self-destruction. Potentially a source of strength in an increasingly difficult world, they are now in such sad shape that they discourage a society that has no other established institution to turn to in its quest for justice and stability. Reform must begin now and go beyond mere tinkering. A new court building here, a few more judges there, some minor changes in rules, a landmark appellate court decision on some legal technicality—this is all that has happened since Roscoe Pound first began sounding warnings to the bar and the public nearly seventy years ago.

It was with the feeling that something—anything—must be done quickly that the twenty-seven judges of the trial court in Detroit filed an unprecedented suit in 1968 to force Wayne County, Michigan, to provide more clerks, probation officers, and assistants to the court; the judges won an order from a neighboring court directing the county to pay $193,000 for the new personnel. It was with the same impulse, although perhaps with less purpose, that Thomas Motherway, a municipal court judge in Saint Louis, simply dismissed traffic court one day in late 1970, and ordered acquittals in all 192 cases, because the boisterous, overcrowded conditions in the courtroom made it impossible for him to go on in good conscience. "When people have to come to court under conditions which are laughable," he said, "nothing can be accomplished." That sense of frustration also led to the surprise resignation of the widely respected Judge Simon Silver of New York's Criminal Court in 1969. These actions may appear to be extreme or bizarre. But the fact is that those few trial court bureaucrats who still aspire to do justice have come to the point where they no longer know how else to respond.

A similar sense of urgency led Chief Justice Burger to decide that, during his tenure on the Supreme Court, he would personally use his high office to assume national leadership in the struggle for court reform. And it is time now that the rest of us, lawyers and other citizens, bend our wills, too, in a methodical but determined attack on the dilemma of our courts. The problem must be approached as the crisis in national survival that it has most surely become.

We must turn from arguing over irrelevant appellate court decisions and legal theories to doing something about the way the law actually works, or fails to work, in reality every day for millions of Americans. We must stop pinching pennies on court finances while allowing the far greater expense of crime, disorder, and citizen dissatisfaction to mount. We must stop treading lightly on lawyers' toes. We must begin instead to entertain and act on suggestions for radical reform.

Just such suggestions are now beginning to appear with unprecedented abundance from a new breed of legal researchers who do not fear questioning entrenched tradition or bringing scientific methods of inquiry and sociological viewpoints to bear on studies of court problems. Thus far, however, their findings have been presented to the legal community in piecemeal form—in the reports of Presidential commissions on the causes and remedies of crime and violence and such studies of law professors, largely financed by philanthropic foundations, as those by Jerome Carlin on lawyers' ethics and the legal problems of the poor, Harry Kalven and Hans Zeisel on the causes of court delays and the workings of the American jury process, Robert Keeton and Jeffrey O'Connell on automobile accident litigation and insurance, and Herbert Packer on the treatment of many kinds of social problems as crimes. Many lawyers still are not familiar with the majority of these new court reform studies, and the general public has been acquainted with almost none of them. Only sporadic press discussion of the Presidential commission studies of crime and violence and the speeches on court reform by Chief Justice Burger and a few other lawyers and judges have reached many citizens.

The suggested reforms for specific problems reviewed in previous chapters of this book have been drawn from existing studies, as well as from the private counsel of reform-minded lawyers. The most urgent bear repeating. They are: (1) reorganization of local trial courts to end jurisdictional confusion and unequal resources; (2) the abandonment by judges and lawyers of archaic delay-producing procedures; (3) the modernization of the machinery of the courts with professional management and such technology of today as computers; and (4) the restructuring of the legal profession and the law schools to channel more and better-trained lawyers, judges, and supporting personnel into the trial courts. All these reforms have gained increasing support over the past year even from within the legal profession, thanks in great part to the leadership of Chief Justice Burger.

Still more needs to be done, however. The courts should be more accessible and more responsive to more citizens. Ways must be found to provide inexpensive legal counsel for working-class and middle-class citizens, as well as for the very poor. Changes must be made in laws and court procedures that give the rich, landlords, merchants, creditors, and government interests unequal advantage over working men, renters, debtors, consumers, welfare recipients, and the poor in general.

Despite strong opposition from lawyers who do not want to lose any business, there is growing interest in removing automobile accident litigation from the courts through reform of liability insurance practices. Even wider support is gathering behind efforts to transfer prosecution of minor traffic violations from the courts to local government motor vehicle agencies, to remove the criminal sanction from narcotics use, gambling, drunkenness, and certain sex acts between consenting adults, and to enable citizens to probate uncontested wills, obtain uncontested divorces, and buy and sell real estate without required legal representation. These changes would eliminate much congestion in the courts, but, more importantly, they would in most cases almost certainly bring about more equitable and sensible handling of these problems and transactions. Typical of the surprising new sympathy for some of these suggestions was the opinion stated by Philadelphia police commissioner Frank Rizzo in a television interview in late 1970 that narcotics addicts "are sick people and should be treated." Rizzo, known as one of America's toughest and most outspoken lawmen, said, "I do not believe that a person should be punished for being an addict . . . or an alcoholic."

Finally, a very few voices in the legal community have also urged that even basic substantive court procedures that have long been taken for granted should be reviewed critically and possibly changed, no matter how deeply rooted they may be in the Anglo-American legal tradition. Everything done in the courts, they argue, should be held up to merciless scrutiny.

For instance, can much of the paper work and many formal requirements and courtesies now encumbering litigation be dispensed with? Many court papers that must be filed, waiting periods that must be endured, and minor procedural steps that must be observed appear to be unnecessary and could be scrapped, thus speeding up the court machinery with no damage in due process.

Should juries be abolished, at least in civil cases? Innumerable studies show that too many jurors are unequal to their task, especially in complicated and tedious civil controversies. Generally, the jurors appear merely to follow the lead of the judge. Often, a case is taken out of the jury's hands for technical reasons, anyway, despite the time invested in selecting, impaneling, and guiding the jurors. In England, where the tradition of trial by jury originated, juries have been abolished for most civil litigation. It would, of course, be a much sharper break with our legal heritage and beliefs to dispense with juries in criminal cases, and there are compelling arguments to be made for allowing a man to be judged by a unanimous panel of his peers before his freedom is taken away. The reform called for in this instance would seem to involve finding ways to improve jury selection and preparedness for criminal cases. Certainly, juries should be more representative cross-sections of the community, and fewer citizens should be excused from service than at present. Rudimentary tutoring in criminal-trial process should be provided for each prospective juror on the first day of his term.

Is our adversary system of litigation barbaric—and counterproductive? Opposing lawyers work more to win victory for their side than to seek truth. Witnesses are primed for testimony by one side and misled on cross-examination by the other. Pertinent evidence is purposely suppressed. Lying by witnesses is commonplace and tolerated. At the same time, each side and the judge must observe every appropriate technicality; a mistake leads to a lost case, and there often is no opportunity to correct even an inadvertent oversight. Lawyers frequently carry on in the manner of the worst ham actors, while judges interject their personal feelings into a case by nuance or outright prejudicial statements. Constant back-and-forth and jigsaw-puzzle presentation of the evidence often leaves jurors baffled at the end of the trial, only to have their minds further scrambled by overly emotional, completely one-sided, and often distorted summary arguments by each lawyer. It is because the cause of justice often seems obscured by these and other shabby exhibitions of legal combat that respected legal authorities fail to condemn such short cuts as the bargained guilty plea.

But should plea bargaining, as it works in most courts today, be maintained and institutionalized? The process now
is as indecorous as fish-market haggling, and subject to
much abuse. Pressure is applied to negotiate some kind of
plea to avoid a trial without regard to whether justice is
being served. Some lawyers have suggested fitting out the
plea-bargaining process with the trappings of due process:
supervision by a judge to be sure the defendant's rights are
being protected, consideration of the tailoring of the sentence in a realistic way to meet the rehabilitation needs of
the offenders, and provision of appellate review for all pleas
later challenged by defendants.

Should not all criminal sentences be reviewed by appellate courts or special multijudge panels empowered to
correct injustices? Trial judges, operating under almost unchecked power to fix sentences as they see fit, often work
great injustices by failing to investigate thoroughly the background of each defendant and the possibilities of available
rehabilitation appropriate to him and instead succumb to
emotional reactions or arbitrarily follow a pet sentencing
pattern. The reform in this field would also mean abolition
of all minimum-sentencing laws, as Chief Justice Burger has
urged, because they severely restrict judges in many states
and create inequities from state to state. Some judges have
also suggested that each court set up a sentencing panel of
two or three judges to fix sentences—deliberately *after* other
judges have conducted criminal trials.

In general, as Yale Law School Professor Daniel J. Freed,
a former court reform specialist for the U.S. Justice Department, has pointed out, much more study is needed of the
"nuts and bolts" of court operations. "It is easy for us to
identify problems," Freed told this writer, "but very difficult
to decide what to do about them." Freed says there is a
need for "social engineering" in the court system—which he

defined as the process of deciding what social or legal purpose one wishes a particular court operation to accomplish and then finding out how best it can be accomplished, regardless of what the past pattern has been.

But Freed and many other leading advocates of court re-form warn that no reform should be tried precipitously, without careful study of the effects of each change on the over-all system. Some of the short cuts that have already been used repeatedly in the courts, such as forced plea bargaining in criminal cases, have produced undesirable results without necessarily always easing the crush on the system.

However, the careful consideration that should be given each suggested reform should not be used as an excuse for shying away from the responsibility of taking some action. Actual change may have to come slowly, but the commitment to study and experiment with change must be immediate and firm. We cannot afford to stand still any longer.

Even with the leadership of the Chief Justice of the U.S. Supreme Court, it will not be easy to make sweeping court reform the kind of compelling national quest that, for instance, put a man on the moon. In addition to the self-protective resistance of much of the legal profession and the apathy of the rest of the citizenry, there will doubtless be a general reluctance to question or change legal traditions that have become a part of our culture even though they may produce no assurance of justice and are not even based on constitutional directives—such as the notion of what constitutes a crime or the tradition of having all legal disputes decided by a jury of twelve fellow citizens.

Much of the change will have to be effected politically. But such change can easily be frustrated. Will politicians risk losing popularity among constituents by voting to legalize narcotics possession, gambling, prostitution, drunkenness, or homosexual activity? Will the majority of legislators who are also lawyers turn their backs on self-interest to help

achieve changes bitterly opposed by the bulk of their profession? Will politicians in influential positions of power and
the party bosses who helped put them there gladly give up
the privilege of deciding who becomes a judge or a court
clerk?

The problem facing the ordinary American, who now
complains that the laws and courts do not seem to work
right, is threefold. He must be willing to spend the money
to make significant improvements in the local trial courts.
He must force lawyers and legislators to realize that court
reform must come and persuade them to work to change the
laws and court procedures accordingly. And, to accomplish
the latter, he must inform himself of and involve himself in
what goes on in his local courthouse.

In *The Courts, the Public, and the Population Explosion,*
edited by Harry W. Jones, contributors Glenn R. Winters
and Robert E. Allard, of the American Judicature Society,
pointed out:

> At some time in American history there may have been a gen-
> eral understanding of the critical role of the judiciary as the
> final rampart for personal freedom and public welfare. If so,
> it was before the onslaught of industrialization, urbanization,
> impersonalization, and population explosion in the first half
> of the twentieth century. Today, courtrooms are as empty of
> informed spectators as school textbooks are empty of informa-
> tion about the operation of justice under law.

It is not enough for worried Americans to lock their doors,
buy guns, complain about Supreme Court decisions, or, conversely, to criticize those who do. It is not enough to complain that the law is wrong, the courts are unresponsive, the
judges lazy, and the lawyers greedy.

It is time instead for citizens to go down to the local
courthouse, look around, and learn to understand what hap-

pens there and then, perhaps, to go to the local bar association or form a committee to ask questions about what is wrong in the court and demand satisfactory answers and reforms. The many new "public service" law firms being organized by bright young lawyers who want to bring about social change through legal, nonviolent means might be interested in bringing taxpayers' suits to force reforms in the trial courts. Certainly, if enough citizens made clear their concern—as they have done on the problem of pollution, for instance—local, state, and national politicians could be convinced that they had better explore and act on court reform if they wish to remain in office.

To accomplish this, it is necessary to make court reform one of the great domestic issues of the 1970's. Those people now deeply concerned about crime, racial injustice, pollution, poverty, and the exploitation of consumers will have to be brought to realize that little can be done to treat these ills unless the nation's trial court system is first made to function well and respond to injustice. The Rule of Law will not exist for any group of aggrieved citizens until the judicial system once again works properly. We must resolve now to begin the difficult task of re-establishing justice in our trial courts and making the law work, as it should, for all Americans.

Bibliography

Advisory Committee on Sentencing and Review, American Bar Association Project on Minimum Standards for Criminal Justice. *Sentencing Alternatives and Procedures.* New York: Institute of Judicial Administration, 1967.

BEDFORD, SYBILLE. *The Faces of Justice.* New York: Simon & Schuster, 1963.

BLOOM, MURRAY TEIGH. *The Trouble With Lawyers.* New York: Pocket Books, Simon & Schuster, 1970.

BLUMBERG, ABRAHAM S. *Criminal Justice.* Chicago: Quadrangle, 1967.

BLUMFELD, F. YORICK. *Congestion in the Courts.* Washington, D.C.: Editorial Research Reports, 1960.

BOTEIN, BERNARD, and GORDON, MURRAY A. *The Trial of the Future: Challenge to the Law.* New York: Cornerstone Library, Simon & Schuster, 1963.

CAMPBELL, JAMES S.; SAHID, JOSEPH R.; and STANG, DAVID P.; eds. *Law and Order Reconsidered: A Staff Report to the National Commission on the Causes and Prevention of Violence.* New York: Praeger, 1970.

CARLIN, JEROME E. *Lawyers' Ethics.* New York: Russell Sage Foundation, 1966.

CARLIN, JEROME E.; HOWARD, JAN; and MESSINGER, SHELDON L. *Civil Justice and the Poor: Issues for Sociological Research.* Berkeley: Center for the Study of Law and Society at the University of California, Berkeley. (Published by the Russell Sage Foundation, 1968.)

CHAMBLISS, WILLIAM J. *Crime and the Legal Process.* New York: McGraw-Hill, 1969.

CIPES, ROBERT M. *The Crime War.* New York: New American Library, 1966.

DACEY, NORMAN F. *How to Avoid Probate.* New York: Crown, 1966.

DAVIS, KENNETH CULP. *Discretionary Justice: A Preliminary Inquiry.* Baton Rouge: Louisiana State University Press, 1969.

Department of Justice, Commonwealth of Pennsylvania. *Report of the Attorney General on the Investigation of the Magisterial System*. Harrisburg, Pa., 1965.

FRANK, JEROME. *Courts on Trial: Myth and Reality in American Justice*. Princeton, N.J.: Princeton University Press, 1949. New York: Atheneum, 1963.

JONES, HARRY W., ed. *The Courts, the Public, and the Population Explosion*. New York: The American Assembly, 1965.

KALVEN, HARRY, JR., and ZEISEL, HANS. *The American Jury*. Boston: Little, Brown, 1966.

KAMISAR, YALE; INBAU, FRED E.; and ARNOLD, THURMAN. *Criminal Justice in Our Time*. Charlottesville: University of Virginia Press, 1965.

KEETON, ROBERT E. *Venturing to Do Justice*. Cambridge, Mass.: Harvard University Press, 1969.

KEETON, ROBERT E., and O'CONNELL, JEFFREY. *After Cars Crash: The Need for Legal and Insurance Reform*. Homewood, Ill.: Dow Jones-Irwin, 1967.

LEVITAN, SAR A. *The Great Society's Poor Law: A New Approach to Poverty*. Baltimore, Md.: Johns Hopkins Press, 1969.

MAYER, MARTIN. *The Lawyers*. New York: Harper & Row, 1967. New York: Dell, 1968.

MENNINGER, KARL. *The Crime of Punishment*. New York: Viking, 1968.

National Commission on the Causes and Prevention of Violence, Staff Report. *Law and Order Revisited*. Washington, D.C.: Government Printing Office, 1969.

National Defender Project. *Report to the National Defender Conference*. Washington, D.C.: National Legal Aid and Defender Association, 1969.

NEWMAN, DONALD J. *Conviction: The Determination of Guilt or Innocence Without Trial*. Boston: Little, Brown, 1966.

OAKS, DALLIN H., and LEHMAN, WARREN. *A Criminal Justice System and the Indigent: A Study of Chicago and Cook County*. Chicago: University of Chicago Press, 1968.

PACKER, HERBERT L. *The Limits of the Criminal Sanction*. Stanford, Calif.: Stanford University Press, 1968.

President's Commission on Law Enforcement and the Administration of Justice. *The Challenge of Crime in a Free Society*. Washington, D.C.: Government Printing Office, 1967.

SCHUR, EDWIN M. *Our Criminal Society: The Social and Legal Sources of Crime in America*. Englewood Cliffs, N.J.: Prentice-Hall, 1969.

SILVERSTEIN, LEE. *Defense of the Poor in Criminal Cases in American State Courts*. 3 vols. Chicago: American Bar Foundation, 1965.

SUBIN, HARRY I. *Criminal Justice in a Metropolitan Court.* Washington, D.C.: Government Printing Office, 1966.

TEN BROEK, JACOBUS, ed. *The Law of the Poor.* San Francisco, Calif.: Chandler, 1966.

United States Department of Justice. *Proceedings of the Attorney General's Conference on Court Congestion and Delay.* Washington, D.C.: Government Printing Office, 1958.

VIRTUE, MAXINE BOORD. *Survey of Metropolitan Courts.* Ann Arbor: University of Michigan Press, 1962.

Walter E. Meyer Research Institute of Law. *Dollars, Delay and the Automobile Victim.* New York: Bobbs-Merrill, 1968.

Index